UNMASKING
Purpose

MEGAN BRUINERS

UNMASKING
Purpose

INSPIRED
PUBLISHING

Unmasking Purpose
First Edition, First Impression 2020
ISBN 978-1-990961-44-1
Copyright © Megan Bruiners

Published by:
Inspired Publishing
PO Box 82058 | Southdale | 2135
Johannesburg , South Africa
Email: info@inspiredpublishing.co.za
www.inspiredpublishing.co.za

CONTENTS

DEDICATION

This book is dedicated to my late Father, Peter Jurd who put his dreams on hold, and to every person living in shame and darkness, afraid to tell his or her story.

ACKNOWLEDGEMENTS

My mother, Sharon Elizabeth Jurd, for pushing me towards my destiny; My sister, Alicia Sharon Fortuin, for believing in all my concepts;

My husband, David Anthony Bruiners, who always believed in me; My future children of destiny who will read this one day;

My destiny helpers assigned to me;

My spiritual oversight: Apostle Taswell Alexander and Prophetess Edwina Alexander;

My spiritual mentor, Ps Chana Richards, for praying me through; Darren August for igniting my dream, and the Inspired Publishing team; and finally,

My Heavenly Father who is the co-author of my story.

INTRODUCTION

A Coronavirus (Covid-19) pandemic has hit South Africa and the rest of the world; and at the time of writing this South Africa is in day 20 of our national lockdown which started at midnight on 26 March 2020. Our President, Cyril Ramaphosa, placed all South African citizens in lockdown to self-isolate in their homes in order to save lives and prevent the virus from spreading. The World Health Organisation (WHO) asserted that the Covid-19 virus spreads primarily through droplets of saliva or discharge from the nose when an infected person coughs or sneezes, therefore it is important to protect yourself by frequently washing your hands or using an alcohol based sanitizer, and not touching your face.

To date (15th April) 2415 people have contracted the virus, 27 have died, and these numbers are increasing day by day. The lockdown was ini- tially to last 21 days but was extended for another 14 days in an attempt to flatten the rising curve of cases. This is a situation in which many people have lost hope, beliefs are being tested, and we all are forced to revisit our spiritual foundations, discover what our purpose is, and assess the extent of our faith. The premise of this book is to assist the readers to find direction in the midst of a detour in their lives.

When we face a crisis or a storm, it provides God with the opportunity of reminding us of His promises. It is not comfortable to be in a storm, but there are valuable lessons there that shape you before the storm clears and you are able to see again. When an aircraft is flying through turbulent weather, the captain makes an announcement to the passengers: fasten your seat-belts and remain seated. You take comfort in hearing his voice even though you cannot see what lies ahead. I have seen people clutching their seats until their faces lose colour, people locked up in the restroom unable to move, and others with their heads hitting the ceiling; all the while the flight crew are walking upright as if it's just another day at the office. The only thing you can do in a storm is to sit back and trust that you will arrive safely. God is the captain of your life and His intention is not to harm you but to go with you through every storm.

Everyone has a story to tell that has the potential to set others free. In this book I will share my own personal encounters with God, which led to a spiritual awakening in me and gave me boldness to share my testimony so others could have victory. My prayer is that this book will help you align with your purpose in the midst of trials and that you will allow the *author and finisher of our faith* to co-author your story.

I am a first generation author, kingdom entrepreneur, purpose coach, and prophetess. I am also an avid advocate for restoration in families and generational lines. I believe that if you start something, you might as well finish it. How many of you find it difficult to complete an assignment or to achieve the goals you have set for yourselves? Very often we have allowed ourselves to be indoctrinated by society and social media – and the advice they offer – only to find ourselves stuck in the same old rut.

I want the person who is desperate for a lifeline – who is stuck in sexual sin and addictions – to know what I didn't know when I was trapped in pornography and fornication. The intention of my testimony is not malicious, or to portray anyone in a negative light, or to cause anyone harm. It is expressed through the lens of love, and is an invitation to you to experience God's pursuit of you. It illustrates God's redemptive love and forgiving nature towards His children, reminding us that there is no sin so great that the love of God cannot prevail over it.

The reason that I can be bold is that the grace of God delivered and sanctified me for a greater purpose. If I do not speak my truth, I am doing a disservice to every individual stuck in addictions regardless of their age, faith, denomination, and past mistakes. It's not about me anymore; it's about that person who needs to be set free.

My story began in Bonteheuwel, a 'coloured' suburb on the Cape Flats in Cape Town, South Africa, a suburb known for poverty, gang violence, unemployment, and drug abuse. What most people fail to realise, though, is that Bonteheuwel is also rich with people who are filled with hopes, dreams, and the potential for purpose and destiny. Yet, living with beliefs tainted by our cultures, traditions, and a mentality of 'this-is-the-way-it-has-been- done-in-past-generations', incurs fear of the unknown, and hinders us from fully realising our capabilities. How many of us find ourselves living below our true potential and leaving this earth with dormant spiritual gifts?

For me, growing up had its own challenges as I struggled with insecurities, low self-esteem, repressed anger, and rebellion against my parents most of my teenage years. My parents had their brand of expressing love and it emanated from what was passed down to them from previous generations. Family dynamics play a big role in how you adapt to, and overcome, the circumstances you are faced with, but it is up to each individual to face his or her fears and trust God for restoration in the midst of brokenness.

My intention with this book is to break the barriers arising from a defeated mindset and to inspire others to get unstuck, be the change they want to see, and pave the way for future generations to experience true liberty. The spiritual foundation of that process rests on the power of God's eternal love for us. My views are not based on religion but on having a personal relationship with God. My own experiences highlight the fact that we are all in need of a Saviour if we are seeking to know our God-given purpose and to fulfil it. If I had allowed the oppression that my forefathers experienced and thoughts of unworthiness to dictate my ability to write, I would have been a generational thief because others would have written my history and their perceptions of my experiences for me.

My Kingdom mandate is to assist in changing the narrative of fear, sexual promiscuity, and addictions in our communities into a narrative of overcoming sexual sin, honouring the covenant with God, and unlocking purpose. However, nothing can happen in your life until you start to believe. You first have to change your beliefs in order to change your behaviour. This book will help you believe that you can unlock your hidden potential, and it will give you guidance on how to unwrap the gift that is inside of you. It is necessary to be transparent and brutally honest about where we find our- selves, in order to move forward in our journey towards wholeness and to go where others won't dare to go. God has written your script from scene to scene and season to season, with the purpose of setting in motion the vision for your life. Everything that happens to you is your personal story and you get to tell it. It's your truth. Your version of it. In your own authentic voice. You are not the victim; you are the victor.

This book is intended to be a transformational tool: for millennials and parents of young adults, both men and women, between the ages of sixteen and thirty five, to enable them to pursue, discover, and live out their purpose, and for any individuals struggling with shame and addictions who want to experience true freedom. To achieve that end, and to help lead the readers on their own journeys, the book is in three parts:

PART I details my personal story of addiction and behavioural aberrations, and uncovers the truth of God's original design for sex and the issue of sexual sin. It breaks the silence over pornography and addictions that are particularly rampant in this global crisis, and provides the means of overcoming them. It also discusses approval addiction and how it prevents us from fulfilling our purpose.

PART II relates my personal testimony and the testimonies of others' breakthroughs, and describes the pitfalls to destiny, in our journeys towards purpose. These illustrate the transforming power of a love encounter with God, His unconditional love, and His saving grace. You will be guided on a journey of self-discovery and of igniting buried dreams.

In **PART III** I delve into my own journey of pursuing entrepreneur- ship, and invite you to also take up your position, armed with a Kingdom mandate, in order to be a co-worker with God. This section assists in unveiling the gifts that every person carries inside of them, gives some Kingdom keys to unlock your God-given purpose, and gives Kingdom keys to aspiring entrepreneurs who need guidance on where and how to get started. As a bonus, you will be equipped with the tools to create your own vision board and track your progress on a uniquely designed PURPOSE MAP! You are then rewarded with a blueprint of a "God-given Purpose Strategy" (GPS) that can be implemented immediately to afford you the opportunity to live a purpose-driven life.

PART 1

UNVEILING SECRET SINS

Chapter One

DATING YOUR FEARS AND INSECURITIES

For God did not give us a spirit of timidity or cowardice or fear, but [He has given us a spirit] of power and of love and of sound judgement and personal discipline [abilities that result in a calm, well-balanced mind and self-control]. (2 Timothy 1:7, AMP)

Beginnings

I was birthed into a generational line of strong yet disadvantaged women who did not have many career options during the apartheid regime. My great grandmother, Elizabeth, loved baking and was very active in the church. My grandmother, Elaine, left school at Grade 9 to help her mother, and was a domestic worker for a priest in an affluent suburb in Cape Town. My mother, Sharon, had the opportunity to study through the post to become a teacher. She went on early retirement at the age of thirty seven and spent the following years caring for and nurturing her family. Her love of reading was birthed when her mother started bringing magazines home that she received from her employer. I developed a love of reading at the age of four, when, engulfed in the reading material around the house, I was taught to spell and read around the living room table. The driving force behind my mother's strict demeanour and persevering attitude was for her children to have the opportunities she never had, and to excel.

My mother did not grow up with the words "I love you" or with hugs and kisses. She was dedicated to making sure that the household chores were done, and she excelled in cooking and baking. My mother carries her age gracefully today. Her love language is through her caring and giving. She possesses undoubted gifts of giving and hospitality.

All these woman figures in my life had a fighting spirit and a will to survive in order to provide a better future for their children.

My father, a local bus driver, enjoyed being in the company of his friends and used alcohol to numb his childhood pain which left behind a residue of guilt and self-condemnation. He never knew who his father was and this meant that he never dealt with any unresolved issues and strongholds. A stronghold is an erroneous pattern of thinking or false belief that creates a false narrative in our hearts. We all have strongholds in our mind where the false belief creates anger, fears, and offenses. Nevertheless, my father had a kind heart and a quiet strength about him, and he was passionate about serving the elderly in our community. He had the patience to listen to everyone's problems in his circle of friends, even though he was battling with his own internal struggles. He was not too keen on expressing his feelings and showing affection because of his childhood and past mistakes. As he and I bonded in our relationship, I had to be intentional in asking the right questions to get the answers I wanted from him.

I have a married younger sibling who is more of an introvert than I. When we were younger, my father would double wrap our Christmas presents in newspaper, making them difficult to open, which left us scrambling to see who opened one first. It turned out to be the most exciting time of the year. Loads and loads of newspaper would be scattered all over the floor. Our peals of laughter were an expression of the love between a father and his two precious girls.

I attended a primary school close to where we lived and was later enrolled at a high school in an affluent suburb called Newlands, which had extra-mural activities and facilities that local schools did not have. I enjoyed studying, but I knew instinctively that I should not disappoint my parents and that it was now or never to make them proud as a token of my appreciation that their hard work was not in vain.

I studied for my diploma in the year 2002 at Cape Peninsula University of Technology (CPUT) which was a Technikon at the time. I excelled in travel and tourism which eventually became my passions, lasting till today.

Dating and Addiction

In the community in which I was raised, I would be walking from the shop and the next minute I would be diving onto hard cement trying not to be hit by a stray bullet. The sight of people somersaulting over one another when running away from a shooting incident in fear of their lives, was my reality when growing up. Teenage pregnancy became a norm. If you dated a gangster you were deemed popular and a big achiever because he was always dressed to impress. If you were not wearing the latest brand name clothing, you would not be able to sit with the cool kids. I would empty out my closet and spend hours in my room deciding what to wear. It was a strenuous task and gave me headaches on a good day. It was an attempt to fit in. I suffered from an inferiority complex every time my hair was not done, or if a particular outfit didn't match well. It was all rooted in having an unresolved identity crisis.

When you have not received a revelation of your identity, you pretend to be someone else. You strive to be like everyone else in order to accept yourself. Only now do I understand the obsession about wearing the latest name brands.

The first time I knew that I liked someone from the opposite sex, and experienced my first kiss, was at the age of fourteen. His name was Ralton, and he was a year older than I. He had a charm about him, a soft voice, and a unique way of doing his hair, combed to one side. He came to visit once, and my mom sat down with us, wanting to know what his intentions were. She mentioned that we were way too young to date. Needless to say, that was the last time I saw him. I still laugh about it as if it happened yesterday. I started dating again at the age of eighteen and was negatively influenced by friends during my first year of studies at university. All I was concerned about, at that time, was having a good time drinking, smoking and experimenting with drugs on weekends. I was not considering the consequences, I so badly wanted to fit in. This was to my own detriment as I began engaging in sexual activities during this time. I neglected to think about my future and my true identity. I couldn't think further than the circumstances I was in. I was lost, controlled by the lusts of my flesh, and stuck in approval addiction.

I excelled in my studies during my first year at university, but I was struggling with lust because of the door of sexual perversion that I had opened. Ungodly soul ties were formed with men I was never destined to marry. This affected my view of sexual intimacy and what God intended it to be in marriage. When you partake in pre-marital sex you become one with each other in every sense of the word: physically, but even more so spiritually. Sex is intended for marriage and becomes dangerous when it is not exercised in that sacred covenant between two people. This is how an ungodly soul tie is formed. We live in a society in which it has become acceptable to indulge in sexual activities outside the commitment of marriage, which is a moral institution that God has designed for us to protect us.

The feelings of brokenness, hurt, and disappointment were my daily experience. They became a part of me. I was searching for love in all the wrong places with approval as my drug addiction. I felt consumed and controlled by negative thought patterns. My fear of rejection was the root cause of not trusting anyone. I was afraid of getting hurt and of the possibility of being disappointed. My walls of defensiveness were as high as the Great Wall of China, not allowing anyone to come close enough to hurt or reject me. Well, at least that is what I thought. I was afraid of being judged. I was afraid of people's opinions, and I was just afraid of being myself. I knew I needed help and that I had to talk to someone.

It is important to identify the source of the fears and insecurities that keep you trapped in the cycle of sex for acceptance, and that hinder you from stepping out of that cycle in faith. True and meaningful love still exists. Many women I have encountered on my journey attribute their low self-esteem and struggles with broken relationships to having 'daddy issues' – an absent father or no father-daughter relationship at all. This opened the door for the enemy to present a counterfeit representation of love which led to a false identity and to soul wounds.

At the age of nineteen, I was seeking validation, affirmation, and purpose for my life. On the outside it looked as if I had it all together, but I was dying inside. During my second year at university, I was tasked to select a tourism establishment for my in-service practical training. My lecturer recommended a few game reserves, and Tsitsikamma National Park, which is on the Garden Route, resonated with me. I had to complete my practical assignment at the National Park for six months to prove my competence, before I could graduate towards my final year for a national diploma in travel and tourism.

The time arrived to start my first day at the Park and my parents dropped me at the student house before they returned home to Cape Town. At this stage I even wondered if I had made a mistake in leaving home and attempting to conquer my fears, although in my deepest being I knew it had to be done. The reality was that my parents had no control over my decisions and just maybe, a change of environment might steer me in the right direction. Epic fail!

The decisions I made with respect to engaging in pre-marital sex during my days as a student, were reckless and worsened my issues. Deep down inside of me something was missing. What was I thinking? That was the problem. I wasn't thinking at all! Amidst the battlefield in my mind, I thoroughly enjoyed the new experiences and the people I met in the Park. I worked at the Information Centre and the scenic view of the ocean was mesmerizing. During my stay in Tsitsikamma, which means 'place of abundant waters', I developed a love for nature. My hobbies became walks in the forest, canoeing, and bird watching. Then, one evening at a party in the student house, I met my husband David. Yes, there was never a dull moment. He had dyed his hair blonde, had charming dimples, an intriguing smile and sported a piercing though his eyebrow. We became friends and God knows why we never pursued one another when we first met. If we had, however, it would certainly have just been a hot mess! I ended up dating his friend which didn't last long before I had to return home.

The six months came to a close and, at the end of 2003, my parents fetched me at the student house. During the long drive home I was trying to process everything. The broken cycle I was in had led me into a repetitive pattern of fear of rejection because of not trusting anyone.

When we are not walking in sexual purity, we attract the things that are not good for us. The temporary satisfaction to appease our sexual appetite overshadows the danger of what we are opening ourselves up to spiritually. We are literally playing with fire when we are controlled by addictive habits or behaviours. It starts with experimentation, then we give it permission to control us, and before we know it, we are caught in full blown perversion. The enemy uses what God intended to be pure to lure us into all kinds of addictions. If you are dating and in a relationship, sex with your future spouse is always worth waiting for. It is simply not worth the heartache and pain to give in to lust. Lust is impulsive and destructive. Love always waits.

The scripture I kept meditating on at the time was, *The fear of man brings a snare, but whoever trusts in and puts his confidence in the Lord will be exalted and safe.* (Proverbs 29:26, AMP). The truth of this scripture, however, did not become a reality to me until years later.

The men I ended up dating in my twenties were either battling drug or alcohol addiction, suffering from depression, or struggling with post- traumatic stress disorder. They all had one thing in common: a way with words. They would tell me what I wanted to hear. I had not yet learned that you are compromising your worth and soul if you stay in a verbally abusive or toxic relationship. It is a bait of Satan. At first glance you would never suspect what lies beneath the surface, until you are deeply caught. My inability to deal with my own pain attracted individuals in need of healing themselves. When you know better, you are supposed to do better. Apparently, not all the time.

Meet George.

We were in an unhealthy relationship for over two years when I was in my early twenties. George was a policeman and suffered from depression. He wanted a relationship with his father very badly but he was hardly ever at home. I felt more like a counsellor than his girlfriend, and somehow I thought I could fix him. One weekend we went camping on the West Coast and we got into an argument in the middle of the night. He made his way out of the tent and ran to the end of the cliff. I heard a loud bang. It sounded like a gunshot fired up into the air. He then hurried back and started packing up everything, saying "We need to leave." I was numb at this point. As we were driving home he put the gun on his lap and stared at me blankly. We never spoke a word for the duration of the drive. The bullet he had fired a few minutes previously was either to scare me or to release his anger. He needed help.

As time went by, George's mother informed me that he was using drugs and stealing her credit card to support his addiction. Our relationship ended shortly afterwards.

God placed a hedge of protection around me to be a testimony to many individuals stuck in broken relationships. It could have played out so differently, yet God kept me. You have to know your worth and love yourself enough to be able to let go of bad relationships that is keeping you from your destiny. An unhealthy relationship breeds instability and turmoil that can be avoided. You need to be healed before you can entrust someone with the responsibility to love you the way you deserve to be loved. You can also only love to the extent you can give love out. It comes from within.

The last toxic relationship I was in, before I started dating my husband for three years, was Clive. He loved driving fast cars and having a good time. On our way home from a party with his friends, I was driving his car. Let's just say that I was in a better condition to drive than he was. I stopped at the traffic lights, and when it was my turn to go, a company vehicle jumped the traffic light, drove into us, and then fled the scene. Clive's car was a write-off. Apart from a few bruises and some discomfort, we survived the collision. He bought a faster car with a turbo engine after that accident, and a few months after that, I discovered that he had cheated on me with his ex-girlfriend. He was supposed to pick me up at work one day and did not pitch. It turned out he was at the movies with her. My heart was shattered. It took me a while to trust again.

If soul wounds are not dealt with, they linger on and cause division, because of the broken filters of our past. When we are led by our emotions, we become defeated. I attributed my irresponsible behaviour to my lack of understanding of my true identity and the purpose of my existence. I was not intentional about living a purpose-driven life.

At the age of twenty six, I had been in touch with David for seven years and we were still in contact when our paths crossed again. He was in Cape Town studying to be a paramedic and staying at the student residence. Both of us had come out of broken relationships and were seeking a new beginning. For the first time I could be myself with him. No pretending. He made me laugh again. He listened to me and helped me look at life from a different perspective. There was something about him. He was different.

At this stage in my life, I was learning to forgive others and, more importantly, to forgive myself and deal with my suppressed anger. I overcame the fear of rejection and gradually opened up to David. I thank God for placing him in my life. He broke down my invisible walls. It was a process. I exhaled. I trusted again. However, our relationship didn't come without its own challenges in the beginning. We stayed together for two years before our encounter with God. Our emotional baggage needed to be unpacked. We both had anger issues and God began a good work within us. We journeyed together and God supernaturally healed us when we surrendered our will. Sometimes you have to let go of the expectations of what you think a relationship should look like and take your hands off the controls. God does a better job anyway. Whenever I share my story, it's as if I'm describing someone else. It seems unreal to me today. There is beauty from our brokenness.

If you are a parent standing in the gap for your child or you are a young adult struggling with addictions – you need to know that you can't fill the void of love with lust. Only God can fill that void and make you whole. If only I had known then what I know now. However, it was not part of God's plan to reveal the truth of my true identity at that time. There was a purpose in my pain.

Needing Affirmation

When you don't hear words of affirmation from your parents, it does not mean that they love you less. At some point my parents knew that I was battling with self-esteem issues and insecurities, but dating my fears prevented me from dealing with those issues.

I believe our childhood is a significant contributing factor towards learned behaviour, our belief system, and our self-esteem. Belief is when we accept that something exists and is true. What we hear and see our parents say and do become our values and norms. If you are a parent and you want to change your children's behaviour, change what they see when they are in your presence. They become what they see. Our belief system is also shaped by the environment we are raised in and by our experiences; what we hear said to us repeatedly becomes our truth. The words you speak to yourself and others contain power. They carry weight and can either promote the purpose and destiny for your life, or block you from ever fulfilling your purpose. We are a result of what we confess with our mouth, and there is *life and death in the power of the tongue* (Proverbs 18:21).

My Heavenly Father's voice eventually ended up being louder than the lies and false perception from the enemy, as, deep down, I wanted to be set free from every burden that rested on me. God is in the business of answering our silent prayers and does His best work with broken vessels.

Chapter Two

OVERCOMING PORNOGRAPHY ADDICTION

Surely you must know that people who practice evil cannot possess
God's kingdom realm. Stop being deceived! People who continue to
engage in sexual immorality, idolatry, adultery, sexual perversion,
homosexuality, fraud, greed, drunkenness, verbal abuse, or extortion –
these will not inherit God's kingdom realm. (1 Corinthians 6:9-10, TPT)

Journey from Addiction to Freedom

The word pornography comes from the Greek word porneia. This word occurs twenty five times in twenty four verses in the New Testament. 1 Corinthians 7:2 makes it clear that porneia refers to sexual intercourse and sexual activity. The word appears for the first time in the New Testament in Matthew 5:32. Fornication is referred to as sexual activity before marriage.

The various common ways of getting addicted to pornography are through adult movies and magazines, online streaming, social media platforms and mobile pornography, through an inherited generational habit, and through fornication to name a few. You usually hear about men's struggles with pornography, but many women are addicted too. Pornography is common for young adults. There are even many born again believers who are struggling with pornography addiction, and who are battling to overcome it.

My own addiction to pornography started during my young adolescence. It started with curiosity but became increasingly luring. I would sneak out of my room in the middle of the night and watch PG 18 movies in the early hours of the morning. The movies with adult content religiously played just after midnight when spiritual principalities operate the most. The enemy works in secret and in darkness. I would mute the sound on the television in the living room so as not to wake anyone. It was an attempt to escape my reality. I would find myself making provision to feed the addiction because of the uncontrollable desires. It became an obsession. You start hiding your phone. My pornography episodes occurred more than once, every single day.

Pornography creeps in subtly before it grows into full blown exposure and turns into an addiction. It was like a craving and it was just not going away until I decided to be intentional to formulate a plan for breakthrough. It is more difficult to get free from it than it is to explore it for the first time. Pornography addiction induces you to lie, be isolated, and break trust, in repetitive cycles of betrayal, pain, and living in shame. I struggled to be free from the addiction for years. A voice would convince me that there was nothing wrong with it. That I was just exploring. It was so far from the truth. It was a lie! Many have been deceived into thinking it is innocent. We are defiling our bodies and it is not pleasing to God. Even if everyone around us is doing it, this does not give us the stamp of approval. What's acceptable in the world is not necessarily what God wants for us. He is only protecting us from ourselves.

The addiction to pornographic content crept into my marriage, but my husband's grace covered me because he understood my journey after battling with it himself for years. Viewing porn releases powerful, mood- altering chemicals that literally rewire your mind, until you crave it more than authentic human connections.

Because of our sinful nature we will always be tempted by explicit images. It's a constant battle. No one is exempted from it. Pornography addiction is no respecter of persons and it chooses its victims regardless of gender, age, and nationality. Sexual sin is more than a bad habit, it's the enemy of our soul. It is demonic at its core. Everything gets processed through our soul. God reminds us to guard our hearts and to be selective about the things we meditate on. Unwholesome talk and perverse conversations flow from the inside (our souls) to the outside (our mouths). It is because of this failure to guard our hearts and mouths that many fail to get a breakthrough. God wants to cleanse our hearts and make us blameless before Him. When our hearts are right, God shows up in a mighty way.

Covenant Eyes Ministry's 2020 studies states that 68% of young adult men and 18% of women use porn at least once every week. Another 17% of men and another 30% of women use porn once or twice per month. This means that for 85% of young men and nearly half of young women, watching porn is at least a monthly activity. Furthermore, the same studies have concluded that one in eight online searches is for pornography. Because porn use thrives in secrecy, many church members are trapped in a cycle of sin and shame, thinking that they're the only ones facing this temptation. The studies revealed that 51% of pastors say Internet pornography is a possible temptation, 50% of all Christian men and 20% of all Christian women say they are addicted to pornography, and 75% of pastors do not make themselves accountable to anyone for their Internet use.

Addiction is not our inheritance. It is not confined to marginalised communities and impoverished families. It can manifest itself regardless of faith and denomination, and even among leaders in the church. You have the self-control to say no. As believers we have no business conforming to the world and indulging in its superficial pleasures. God is uncovering hidden things in this new era and He is deploying His prophets to expose the darkness. He is coming back for His spotless Bride – the Church – and we should live ready. This crisis is our wake-up call. We need to flee from sexual immorality as fast as we can.

Furthermore, addictions are a form of escapism which stem from an inner lack or void and they can lead to other types of sexual sin. Sexual sin can be defined as sexual immorality, fornication, or any sexual attitude or behaviour for the benefit of oneself that deviates from God's original design for mankind. It begins as a set-up from the enemy that simulates God's intentions, corrupts them, and presents them packaged as something desirable. The mind then becomes a battlefield. If we do not renew our minds with the word of God, the enemy can control our thinking and prevent us from having a sound mind and making wise decisions. Thoughts of lust and perversion can lead us into temptation, followed by the deception that nothing is wrong with our actions; we then defile our bodies and fall into idolatry. This leaves an opening for the spirit of lust to enter and brings us into bondage. Whatever you can't stop doing is something that masters you. If it's a bad habit or destructive behaviour pattern that controls you, it becomes your master. Whatever you submit to, you are essentially worshiping.

This is why God instructs us to flee from sexual immorality: not only is it an offense and dishonouring to Him who made us for something so much better, it traps us in destructive behaviour patterns, and damages us and our capacity for clean, healthy, and constructive relationships. This is why sexual intimacy outside marriage is against God's will: it affects our intimacy in marriage, and our view of sensual pleasure becomes tainted and held captive by past experiences. When God says we must flee, He is saying: run for your life lest you fall into sin!

Sex is like fire. If you keep it in the fireplace it will keep you warm, but anywhere else in the house it will burn the house down and destroy it. God urges us that if we *burn with passion,* we should commit to the covenant of marriage. Jesus said that if you so much as look at someone with lust, you are committing adultery.

But if you have no power over your passions, then you should go ahead and marry, for marriage is better than a continual battle with lust. (1 Corinthians 7:9, TPT)

There is a need to distinguish between having sexual desires and giving in to lust. Pornography and masturbation increase your appetite to sin in the body and are enslaving. Wherever love is lacking, lust creeps in and tempts its victim into a temporary sexual experience which fails to produce lasting satisfaction. As soon as you awaken your sexual urges outside of marriage, you invite the spirit of lust and perversion. You also create a mental block for the day when it should be explored and enjoyed by you and your spouse. Shame, guilt, and condemnation are close relatives of sexual sin and leave behind deeply embedded scars if not dealt with and uprooted.

We are faced with battles daily, but God has given us a way out for every temptation we are faced with. It is vital to exercise self-control in this area so as to be able to focus and meditate on the things of God and resist the fleshly desires and patterns of this world. We overcome temptations by the power of God's word and following the example of Jesus Christ when He himself was tempted in the wilderness but did not sin. He has also given to us the power to have the victory over all things.

Inherited Trends and Tendencies

Bloodline trends that are passed on to the children in families may persist until the fourth generation. You will find that one family struggles with financial crises and teenage pregnancies while another deals with sexual abuse, adultery, and addictions. God has given us free will. We have the power to choose between life and death, blessings and curses, and to reap the rewards of what was sown: *This day I call the heavens and the earth as witnesses against you that I have set before you life and death, blessings and curses. Now choose life, so that you and your children may live.* (Deuteronomy 30:19, NIV)

If you look closely, you can identify similar traits in members of your family, no matter how far back they are in your genealogy. Such habits may include, but are not limited to, the following:

- most of the men in your family seem to die young,

- marriages do not last in your family,

- members of your family have succumbed to alcohol and drug addiction or a perverse spirit that travelled through a generational line,

- family members fall into sexual sin.

These characteristics and internal struggles speak of spiritual foundations which exist within a family lineage.

Our generations have been robbed through the choices that our forefathers made, which were 'stored in the archives'. Often family members were sworn to secrecy for the fear of being judged and/or exposing a family scandal – *so you nullify the [authority of the] word of God [acting as if it did not apply] because of your tradition which you have handed down [through the elders].* (Mark 7:13, AMP)

You may have, unbeknown to you, inherited a generational trend that makes you more than otherwise vulnerable to certain sins, but if the enemy can isolate you and make you believe that you are the only person addicted to sensual pleasures and experiencing feelings of guilt, then he has a stronghold over your mind. With the increased bombardment from social media, such as pop-up messages inviting you to adult chat groups which prey on the young and vulnerable, and trending TikTok videos making unsupervised youth vulnerable to sexual predators, resistance becomes increasingly difficult. In this new era of Covid-19, there is a virtual world that has been accessed to facilitate communication, business, education, ministry, and personal fulfilment, but it also facilitates other less desirable uses. The digital devil is unseen, but can be a dangerous devil, deceptively luring people into his evil schemes through subtle sexual images, which create an appetite for viewing pornographic content. We need to break the silence, and not only create awareness of these dangers, but provide platforms for both women and men to break free from bondage and self-sabotage. We are not our mistakes. Our identity in Christ supersedes our actions, and sexual sin can be conquered if we keep our eyes fixed on our Abba Father. John Eckhardt wrote,

Sexual sin is one of the hardest sins to break. Many believers struggle with generational lust that has passed down through the family lines. Lust is a demonic substitute for true love. Rejected individuals have a greater chance of being involved in sexual immorality at a young age. Lust is not only sexual but can also manifest in materialism, overindulgence, food addictions, drug and alcohol addictions, and clothing.

If you are a woman or man battling an addiction, your answer is hidden in Jesus Christ, and He connects the dots of your internal struggles to your God-given purpose. You do not have to be enslaved by lustful desires and addictions that keep you from being the best version of yourself as God intended. Will you deny yourself sensual pleasures to follow Jesus? The decisions you make now are acts of worship unto God and will determine where you will spend your eternity. We must no longer bend the truth to satisfy our own flesh.

How Do You Achieve Breakthrough?

After years of living with compulsive addictions and the deception accompanying the addictions, I was still in bondage, even after two attempts to be set free. I was broken and in need of a Saviour. When you are desperate for change and you cry out to God to save you, you get His attention. Finally, two years into our marriage God delivered me from pornography addiction. My transparency here is motivated by the desire to expose darkness and the plans of the enemy, and to see others set free from this addiction. But we need to give Him permission to move on our behalf. He does not force His will upon us. Additionally, it is imperative that we are accountable to someone as we wage war against the father of lies.

Here are a few steps that I personally followed to overcome the silent killer.

Fasting and praying broke the stronghold of my addictions. It should be emphasised that it's only one of the ways one can be set free. One also needs to deal with the issues of self-love and identity. Fasting, for me, opened the door to a deeper, more intimate relationship with God. Fasting is a spiritual discipline that works together with praying and giving, which are three spiritual foundations for every believer. These three disciplines give believers a better chance of winning the battle over addiction. Fasting can be done over a period of one to three days, depending on your health and what you feel led to take on. God does not hold an account of the number of days we fast or the religious acts and laws that we follow. He searches the heart and the motivation behind our fasting and prayer life. Fasting strengthens our inner man and boosts our spiritual growth.

Praise and worship are additional weapons of warfare that destroy the works of the enemy. There is a shift in the atmosphere when you seek God's presence, praise Him for who He is, and offer your worship as a love offering to Him.

Meditating on the word of God and engraving it on your heart transforms and renews your mind. Learn to set boundaries when triggered to watch any inappropriate content, resist all unwholesome thoughts, and refuse them permission to occupy your mind. Triggers can be thoughts, experiences, and feelings that induce a strong desire to engage in addictive behaviour; these may be overtiredness, feelings of being alone, explicit scenes in a movie, sexual content on your mobile device, or merely perverse talk in the company you keep. How frequently are you on social media? Be selective about what you watch. Avoid the triggers by first identifying them. For instance, going online at night is a trigger. Once your sexual appetite is triggered, your mind becomes contaminated with inappropriate images, and it becomes difficult to meditate on pure thoughts. Therefore, it requires a daily decision to be obedient to the word of God. He honours such a decision. Allow God access to your pain and what you are incapable of curing.

Being intentional to pursue your purpose keeps you focused and aligns you to God's will. Any addiction in your life is occupying a space the Lord wants. Whatever you deem more important than spending time with God is idolatry. You are attracted to what stimulates you.

Repentance brings you closer to God as you show true remorse for your addictions. This allows Him space to bring about an inner change of heart, to transform you from displaying wrong behaviour, and to empower you to bear good fruit and overcome any addiction. Repentance means to think again or to change one's mind. Do not condemn yourself if you have not received breakthrough from your addiction after a few attempts. It is a process and if you are reading this you are heading in the right direction. Ultimately, you become what you repetitively think *and* confess.

Seek help and find yourself an *accountability partner* – someone you can trust who will hold you accountable and tell you the truth. Evil prevails when an individual is isolated and things are kept secret. Get a reliable prayer partner; this can be one of your peers or a spiritual covering to intercede in prayer with you. It's a continuous war that consists of many battles. If you are married, be open with your spouse and be transparent about your activities online. As a married couple you have supportive roles to extend grace and accountability to one another. This is what I discovered personally that unlocked my breakthrough.

A pure heart requires you to change how you view the addiction and its consequences. You need to identify what you have allowed to enter your heart, mind, and soul, as well as the environment you exposed yourself to. God cannot heal what you refuse to reveal. Throughout my story I refer to the heart because it is the focal point of our understanding, and the processing of our thoughts and the events in our lives. Filtering the triggers is only a temporary solution. Sexual immorality and wicked thoughts flows out of the hearts of men; and the evil desires comes from within. It is out of the heart that everything flows and your actions follow. *Keep thy heart with all diligence; for out of it are the issues of life.* (Proverbs 4:23, KJV)

The Woman at the Well

When a woman from Samaria who was bound in sexual immorality came to draw water, she met Jesus, who asked her to give Him a drink. He was awaiting her response in order give her what she was longing for: eternal life. Jesus transformed her thinking and what she perceived to be impossible. He told her that the rivers of living water He had to offer her would forever quench her thirst and she would no longer need to look for this thirst-quenching property in another man. The woman was astonished at Jesus's accurate words concerning her when He revealed to her that the man she was living with was not her husband. She left her water jar and went into the city to share this personal encounter with the people. It only takes one moment for God to remove the shame and guilt that you carry around for years. God wants your heart and worship so He can perform a miracle in your life.

When the people brought a woman to Jesus who had been caught in adultery, His response was, *He who is without [any] sin among you, let him be the first to throw a stone at her.* (John 8:7, AMP) Jesus identified both issues in this account: that of the woman's sin and that of her accusers. The woman was instantly set free, both literally and spiritually as Jesus' words empowered her to *sin no more.* He had a purpose for her life. We must be very careful of the standard by which we measure the vessels God chooses for his assignments. What qualifies a leader in the eyes of God is very different from what society today may view as a qualification.

In the year 2015, God instructed me to start a community women's prayer group to create a safe space for women and to arrange outreach programmes for the destitute. At first, the thought of starting this initiative was daunting, but there were skills I had to acquire, confidence that needed to be nurtured, and leadership skills that were developed as I facilitated the group. I felt unqualified, but God reminded me of my silent prayers asking Him to use me. He qualified and graced me to finish what He placed on my heart. It was during this time that I learned to travail in prayer and to intercede for broken women. God spoke to my heart as He was refining me and whispered, "I am working on the minister and not the ministry." It was part of my refining process and I had to be led by His Spirit and not my emotions.

Deliverance from Shame

The enemy knew his time was up. My husband and I made plans to go on a road trip to the Wild Coast in 2016, after spending some time with his parents in Knysna. One of my spiritual mothers, Ma Lynn, whom I had met a couple of years previously, invited me to attend a prayer meeting during the visit to my in-laws. David was helping his father with repairs around the house so I went alone. Ma Lynn has a heart for broken and destitute women. She runs her ministry from her home in Knysna.

One of the pastors of a Christian radio station brought his team through, who needed prayer. This is when I encountered false prophets who prophesied and spoke word curses over me. I immediately nullified the spoken words when I realised what was happening. God was teaching me to discern the spirit at all times and it became the training ground for my ministry that was to come. Any spirit that operates apart from the Holy Spirit, whether it's superstition or divination, is not from God. Deception is a dangerous weapon the enemy uses to distract us. He will attempt to use our past to pull us back into darkness.

The false prophet's house burned down not long after that incident. God covers and protects His children. God has an assignment for our lives, but so does the enemy. He is afraid of our becoming aware of who we truly are. The voice of a sound prophet is critical in this hour to give vision to God's people, His church, and the nations. People perish because of a lack of knowledge. The time has arrived for true prophets to arise and represent Him in the earth.

A year after my encounter with the false prophets, Ma Lynn, in planning a women's conference for more than one hundred and fifty women, entitled "Preparation for the Bridegroom", asked me to be one of the speakers. At first I thought I wasn't ready but the Lord spoke to me and whispered in my ear that I was, and that I would move in His strength and power and not my own. God needs us to be available and we will not always feel ready to do His work. It is He who equips us for the works of ministry.

The countdown to the women's weekend conference began and I was expectant for a move of God. A few months before the conference, in October 2017, I was asked to minister at our local church. I gained the confidence to share my story about my pornography addiction. Some of the believers and leaders were shocked, others stared at me, some in disbelief. I believe there were some who hid behind their own superficial mask. I could see it in on their faces, but they weren't brave enough to utter a word.

The woman's prayer group I had been leading had been growing and twenty three women secured their spots for the camp. I had arranged our transportation, our t-shirts were printed, and the day arrived for our departure to Oudtshoorn. Women took a bus from Willowmore, George, Knysna and surrounding areas, and attendees flew in from Johannesburg. When we arrived at the hotel, there was excitement in the air. I must admit, I was nervous because I was entering unfamiliar terrain. But I told myself that I was going to be bold and courageous for God. I was going to do it afraid. And I did! I was getting accustomed to being thrown into the deep end and finding my way back to shore.

Although there was jealousy and gossip, and there were spiritual attacks in the atmosphere from all directions, God was faithful and assigned destiny helpers to cover me in prayer. God chooses whom He wills, and this time, I was prepared for battle. I saw first-hand how ministry titles became a badge of honour and pride reared its ugly head. I was not moved and stayed focused on my assignment.

The enemy is stubborn and refuses to be exposed, but God already had the victory. He performed a miracle before I preached my message that Sunday. He delivered me from shame and I experienced His supernatural touch as His voice whispered, "You are forgiven". He gave me a 'garment of praise' and released the oil of gladness over me that day. He healed my mind and soul instantaneously from the feelings of shame and condemnation. There was a thick tangible presence of God as I ministered for the first time that Sunday on sexual sin. This event became the stepping stone for the ministry and calling upon my life.

I had prepared on the book of Esther until 2 am that morning but God changed my message at the eleventh hour to minister to women who were in need of a 'spiritual makeover'. I was obedient. The glory of God was in that place. I was buzzing from that experience of the tangible presence of God for months after the woman's camp. Unfortunately, there were women who came back the same, not willing to change. When we do not prepare ourselves spiritually and mentally as we go through transition, we delay our breakthrough.

God saw it fit to surround me with strong Godly women because of the nature of my assignments. Being a vessel of God is a privilege and an honour that I do not take lightly. It is my heartbeat to represent Him well at all times. We should serve Him with excellence in all we do. You can be saved but it does not mean that you have been sanctified. Sanctification is a process of being made holy as you spend time in God's presence.

Overcoming Shame

The heaviest garment a person can ever wear is the garment of shame.

(Johnathan Welton)

Living with shame feels like being suffocated by a force greater than you, as if you are trapped in your own skin, and someone has dumped a ton of bricks on your soul, weighing you down. There is a real enemy roaming around to steal, kill, and destroy the plan God has for your life. Shame is one of his weapons. When you submit to

God, you will gain the strength to resist the devil and he will flee. You need to be fervent in prayer until you see the results. Your spiritual enemy doesn't attack you because you are weak, he attacks you because you have a divine purpose to fulfil.

It is important to note here that it is not God's intention to take away from the pleasures derived from sex in its proper context, that is, within marriage. There is no shame in God's order for us. After all, the scriptures start out with two naked people living in a garden under the command to *be fruitful and multiply*. Sex is a God-idea, when making love in the way He intended.

Chapter Three

APPROVAL ADDICTION

Whatever you do [whatever your task may be], work from the soul [that is, put in your very best effort], as [something done] for the Lord and not for men, knowing [with all certainty] that it is from the Lord [not from men] that you will receive the inheritance which is your [greatest] reward. It is the Lord Christ whom you [actually] serve. (Colossians 3:23, AMP)

During my party days, the only thing I was concerned about was having a good time and feeling a sense of belonging. I would say yes to friends when, deep down, I was struggling with unfulfilled and unmet desires. I wouldn't dare disappoint anyone even though people disappointed me daily. I then had to face the consequences of my actions and take responsibility. God had to deliver me from people's opinions because of the call on my life and the Kingdom assignments with my name on them.

Our purpose is not to please everyone. We have been called to please God, not people. What others think of us is not our business. Opinions are just that; they are not facts. We need to put our minds at ease with the fact that if we don't do what people expect from us, we will not die. Feelings may be hurt in the process, but we will eventually get over it. We will learn to become comfortable with being uncomfortable. The problem with the desire for approval lies in the motive behind pleasing people; it should not be rooted in fear. We should not be lured into popularity with others; they can love us today and judge us tomorrow.

If you can't find the time to prioritize doing the things God expects from you, it may be that you have become preoccupied with proving yourself to people and are thus living an imbalanced life. Many people are familiar with drug addiction and alcohol addiction. However, in the twenty- first century many have succumbed to a condition, triggered by low self- esteem and the fear of people's opinion, called approval addiction. Approval addiction is spurred on by insecurities and feelings of not being worthy.

When you find it difficult to receive gifts from others, to respond with thanks when someone compliments you, and you decline opportunities by making excuses, you are most probably dealing with symptoms of approval addiction that is rooted in rejection and fear. What views about yourself have you allowed to define you? Why is it uncomfortable when someone praises you, or when you feel you don't receive enough praise for an achievement? Can it be that you have not embraced your true identity and the fact that you are destined for greatness? You do not need the permission of certain individuals to walk into your calling and pursue your destiny.

Trying to be anyone but yourself is burdensome and drains your energy, to say the least, because you are not being the authentic version of yourself that God created you to be. A lifestyle of people-pleasing weekends in the club, and pious Sundays in the church, creates a battlefield in your mind, in which you are constantly bombarded with thoughts and emotions that keep you enslaved in guilt, damaging desires, and dashed hopes. It also dishonours God. God does not bless whom we pretend to be.

I want you to know that I understand what you are fighting and that only God's love can pull you through. If you are a parent and your child is showing symptoms of approval addiction, don't judge him or her. On my journey of birthing purpose in women, I have found that some individuals growing up without a father figure have deep-rooted anger, and are tormented with feelings of abandonment and feeling unloved. Fearing to say 'no' and living your life viewed through the lens of inadequacy is the most heart-wrenching thing to do. Whenever you have bad feelings and you replay them in your mind, you punish yourself. Feelings of loneliness may creep in, and you may find yourself adopting an orphan spirit. You can be surrounded by a group of people and still feel lonely. There is a higher purpose for our existence and we should not be caught up with what we experience in the natural, and a preoccupation with who left us.

Transitioning From Toxic Thinking

I remember my transition from toxic thinking to controlling my thinking and how hard the journey was. I had been controlled by mood swings, unhealthy thought patterns, and a broken belief system. One moment I would be happy, and the next I would be in a dark hole fixated on negative emotions. I was far from speaking life into my situation. I was ignorant of the spiritual realm and God's divine plan for my life. God had to work in my heart to enable me to forgive others, by uprooting bitterness and hard- heartedness. I quickly learned that unforgiveness is like drinking poison and expecting the other person to die from it.

I was paranoid and feared being rejected. I could never make eye contact when I spoke to someone. I couldn't handle criticism and had no confidence. I was a social butterfly, yet I did not believe in my own capabilities. I doubted. I was indecisive. I never enjoyed going out to dinner by myself because I did not enjoy my own company. Change started when I decided to be a better version of myself. To live again. To be free from toxic thoughts and focus on the possibilities of where I wanted my life to be. I can honestly say that God's pursuit of me and His reckless love was more powerful than the voice of the enemy. The defining moment came when I started declaring who God says I am, confessing it out loud every day. I bought all of Joyce Meyer's books on the mind and meditated on them together with scripture. I discovered that if you don't like yourself, then it is difficult for others to connect with you. The moment I addressed the feelings of being alone, it made sense that if I did not accept who God created me to be, I sabotaged my growth and fell prey to self-rejection.

I had to be intentional. God's word was sharper than a double edged sword and pierced into the deepest part of my heart. We become who we surround ourselves with, and I had to eliminate the friends that negatively influenced me. Gratifying my flesh was no longer part of my agenda. Negative thoughts may come, however, God has given us the ability to act on the positive ones. It's a mindshift. The constant battle between our soul and our spirit man will always be raging within us. We have the power to choose what is right. Jesus was sent to the earth as a man to show us that it was possible. My desire is to have a deeper and more intimate relationship with the Holy Spirit. What are you willing to leave behind? Who are you prepared to let go?

Seasons

During one of my transitions, after leading the women's group in my local community for more than five years, I felt God pulling at the strings of my heart and leading me to close the group as it had served its purpose.

My season with the women's group ended, and those that grew spiritually branched out into their own respective ministries. One woman forwarded me a message to say that she was hurt that I left and moved onto the next season of my life. I explained to her that the projects could continue and that every woman who had a conviction to do outreaches in the community should do so, if it was in alignment with their purpose. It was never meant to be about one particular person, but about the work that was being accomplished in people's lives in the community, through the group, for a season.

If you do not understand your role in the kingdom, your experience of transitioning will feel like people are leaving you. Be careful when you follow someone else's vision, that you do it for the right reasons and understand your role. Do not idolize the person leading you, but invest your time in tasks that tie in with the unique assignment that was set out for you. Stay true to your convictions.

Your assignments, also, may be seasonal and not everyone will understand this. You need to be obedient to the voice of God and stay within His will. If I had stayed to please people, my next assignment and where God was calling me to would have been delayed. Sometimes it's difficult to let go of the past and move onto the next season or assignment, but it is vital. We should love everyone but not allow their opinions to control us. Our motives are imperative. We should never stay in a situation based on what others think or demand of us. Our obedience is attached to someone else's victory. We will be left behind if we follow the crowds and jump on every bandwagon.

Words of Truth and Affirmation

One of our love languages is words of affirmation. If you want to be affirmed, you will have to give affirmation to receive it. As babies the first words that we utter are "mamma" and "dada" depending on the cultural context we were born into. Parents will anticipate the first words spoken and react with extreme happiness if these endearing words are spoken. As the child grows up, the parent's love and affection grows and they are expressed through words like "I love you" or "I am proud of you". If not, the child will look for affirmation elsewhere because he or she was designed to receive love and give it in return.

It becomes a problem, however, when you need words of affirmation to function and progress, and when you feel unloved if they are not uttered. The very thing you are expecting from someone in any particular relationship, may be the exact thing they never received growing up.

The sooner you realise that your affirmation comes from God, the sooner you can let go of holding others hostage to your expectations of them. I do understand that in abusive homes it is difficult to break through when negative things have been spoken over you by parents and relatives, but you are not defined by your circumstances, you are defined by the design of your Heavenly Father, and you are thus destined to be more than an overcomer.

Decide to speak words of God's truth to yourself and words of affirmation to those around you. The more you do it, the more natural it becomes. We are all wired differently and often mean well, but the subconscious mind has a subtle way of showing us that we have not arrived yet and points towards our soul wounds. Have you ever said things you apologised profusely for later? I have, and I'm sure you have too. Identify any wrong feelings over the need to be reassured, and correct them with the word of God.

The words we speak can cause great harm if they are not intended to edify the person they were meant for. Word curses are potent and destructive.

Whatever people have said about you, whether they are spiritual leaders, teachers, figures of authority or parents, can also be chains that have a grip on you and prevent you from reaching your destiny. May this be the day that you are released from word curses spoken over you that ended up choking your potential. You don't have to be kept hostage by the negative words of others. Also, as a parent, you need to make a commitment to speak life over your children's future self or the enemy will do it. Set yourself free so you and your family can pursue greater things.

Are you Martha or Mary?

Mary and Martha were sisters who opened up their home to Jesus as He travelled. In the presence of Jesus, Martha was too busy to receive from Him while Mary sat at His feet and listened to His wisdom. It appears from this story that Mary was free from approval addiction and unconcerned about people's opinion of her. As a result, she gained revelation, insight, and understanding, while Martha became preoccupied, worrying about the deadlines of meeting the physical needs of the company. (Luke 10:38-42)

The greatest distraction we can succumb to is busyness. There is no need to be busy without a purpose for it. I noticed that Martha was task- orientated while Mary was focused on worshiping and sitting at the feet of Jesus. When we do things with a performance-based mentality instead of nurturing an intimate relationship with the Lord, we tend to miss Him. I had to learn to let go of Martha's pride and embrace the humility of Mary that enabled her to receive from Jesus without feeling guilty.

Will you fully give yourself to breaking free from the stronghold of approval addiction or will you miss the opportunity to be the better and truer you? I believe that Martha neglected to be all that she could be for her unique assignment, because she was too busy. The busyness of Martha comes to visit from time to time; then I have to remind myself to take a deep breath and treasure the moments of fellowship with the Lord.

Five Steps Towards Breaking Approval Addiction

If you want to win over the addiction to approval and conquer your fear of rejection, the following steps that I personally implemented over a period of time, will help you:

1. *Repent for nursing your feelings* of guilt and the desire for approval, and for allowing them to control you; this is nothing short of idolatry. Make a commitment to change and move away from focusing on your emotions. You also need to forgive yourself and those who have hurt you. Condemnation is from the enemy, but conviction comes from God. The moment you stop playing the guilt and blame game, change will knock at

your door. Write down the names of those who have hurt you on a piece of paper, then tear it up as you release their grip over you. It is a process and your "yes" is required to start it. Joyce Meyer stated in one of her books that 'a refusal to forgive our enemies drives a wedge between us and God. It adversely affects our faith, weighs heavily on our conscience, and prevents true worship.'

Over time God has instructed me to ask forgiveness from those who have hurt me. It was one of the most difficult things I ever had to do. I would pick up the phone, make the call, send the text message, or apologise in person, because I was committed to doing whatever it took to be used by God even if it meant swallowing my pride. How the other party reacted was none of my business. The power lies in 'doing it afraid'. Your personal power is your superpower and it should be protected at all times. Do not allow unforgiveness to take root in your heart. Everyone gets offended; however, it does not have to progress into bitterness and strife if we press through past the anger.

2. *Name it and tame it.* Write down why you need the approval and give it a name. Get to the root of the problem:

   I feel rejected because...

   I am overwhelmed by fear because.................................

   I feel I am not good enough because.............................

   I have fear of failure because...

I feel alone when...

Past failures may have caused you to have an inferiority complex so that you see yourself as less than. What are the words you say to yourself when you are alone? The dialogue we have with ourselves is key if we want to win the battle. What have you perceived to be true about yourself that is damaging your self-esteem? Has anyone spoken word curses over you that have become part of your spiritual make up? Negative influences and people in authority might have spoken hurtful things to you that caused an offense in your heart and hindered you from moving forward. Remember that words contain power and can make or break us, but the word of God rebuilds us.

3. *Identify if there is anyone controlling you; or perhaps you are the controller.* Where does it originate from? The biblical meaning of witchcraft is when someone forces his or her will upon you, manipulates you, controls your thinking, and prevents you from making decisions without their influence. Their intention is to influence you to do things their way. You need to break any ungodly soul ties with these individuals and set boundaries for yourself in your relationships going forward.

If you are a student in university and are pressurised by your parents to go into a certain field, you may eventually cave in and end up failing to pursue what God has uniquely set out for you to do. You need to follow your instincts and passions, stand your ground, and communicate to your 'boundary breakers' to respect the limits you have set up. What you do not protect, you neglect.

If you are the controller, you need to seek humility. God exalts the humble and resists the proud. You do not want to be a stumbling block to someone else's progress and burn relationship bridges because of the need to be controlling.

4. *Confront emotions and feelings* that have been triggered, and deal with them, especially when it becomes hard. Confrontation is the scariest thing to do when you fear the unknown. Confide in a friend/mentor to pray with you, and wait for the right time to communicate if there is a person you need to confront. We tend to repeat an incident in our minds that steals our joy. Discern which thoughts you should not entertain, and then cast them down. Intentionally meditate on positive thoughts. Apply self-control and refuse to feed the addiction. *But the fruit of the Spirit is love, joy, peace, forbearance, kindness, goodness, faithfulness, gentleness and self-control.* (Galatians 5:22-26, NIV)

5. Pray for strength in the areas you are weak, and desire the fruit of the spirit so that you can resist, at all costs, the temptation to go back.

Invest time in discovering your true identity in Christ by mediating on who God says you are. This will take you to the next step of living victoriously. Be intentional about encouraging those around you. Don't wait for compliments or for someone to encourage you. Initiate them yourself. Declare aloud the things you want to see changed in your life. There is power in the spoken word. Learn to BE and not just DO. Separate your actions and behaviours from who you are. Trust God in the process. Renew your mind daily by *not conforming to this world [any longer with its superficial values and customs], but be transformed and progressively changed [as you mature spiritually] by the renewing of your mind [focusing on Godly values and ethical attitudes], so that you may prove [for yourselves] what the will of God is, that which is good and acceptable and perfect [in His plan and purpose for you].* (Romans 12:2, AMP)

Be sure to make the right choices – NOT emotional ones – going forward. God is your vindicator and will fight your battles for you.

You have made it thus far! You have embarked on a journey of self-discovery and are about to dig into the transition from struggling with addiction to pursuing an intimate relationship with God and eventually discovering purpose, in the next couple of chapters. If you stay the course you will come out transformed and knocking on the door of destiny waiting on the other side. You may still be in a dark place right now, but there is a light you are drawn to that cannot be dimmed, and it is drawing you closer to who you were created to be. Discontentment is the seed for change, and the reason you are here is beca use you are still searching for answers. I pray that you find your lane and prosper in it as you connect the dots to your purpose.

Chapter Four

CHASING PURITY

*Let no one look down on [you because of] your youth, but be an example
and set a pattern for the believers in speech, in conduct, in love, in faith,
and in [moral] purity.(1 Timothy 4:12, AMP)*

If you are struggling with sexual impurity, an impure heart, and a
lack of spiritual purity, the chances are that you have not fully
embraced your identity in Christ. Purity can be defined as being free
from sexual immorality, or intentionally deciding to have pure
thoughts and intentions by applying self-control. Just because
everyone is doing it does not make it right and acceptable. An
identity shift is needed if you are chasing and embracing spiritual
purity. Johnathan Welton wrote,

Identity is made of three components: the mind, the heart, and revelation. The mind represents all of the thinking that a person has processed. The heart contains all of the experiences that a person has had. Revelation is the place where the heart and mind have come into agreement to form a foundational belief system.

When you think right, you do right! Your identity flows out of a revelation of who you are and who you were created to be. We need to identify attitudes and habits that blur our revelation of who we are.

Pursuing Spiritual Purity

In 1 Peter 1:16 it states that *You shall be Holy (set apart), for I am Holy.*

Spiritual purity (holiness) is not a list of do's and don'ts nor is it rules and regulations. Holiness and righteousness is not what we do but what God declares us to be. To be holy means to be set apart to do His will. When you pray *Our Father who is in Heaven, Hallowed be thy name*, it is because He is holy and His name should be used with reverence towards Him. God is saying that we should not blend in with the rest of the world but strive to reflect His righteousness on earth. Thus, spiritual purity or holiness is a lifestyle. It is more than our outside appearance or the way we dress. It is a heart attitude towards our Saviour that aligns our thoughts, and thus our words and actions, with His character and His ways.

It is a privilege to partake in God's likeness and to be set apart to do His will. He found it fit to look past our sin and choose us even though we were unqualified. You don't have to be perfect and have it all together to accept the invitation to be a child of God. He says come as you are and I will give you rest. Spiritual purity leads us to be in right standing with God and aligned to His purpose. We can justify our actions all we want, yet they may be way off from the direction we are supposed to go. Can it be that the compass that you have been following most of your life has been leading you in the wrong direction? That the counsel you have been receiving was unwise and contributed to where you currently find yourself? You can make it right by allowing God to be a part of your story and unlock your God- given purpose.

It may be that many have judged you based on your mistakes, outside appearance, and capabilities, but God searches the heart. He chooses you based on your heart attitude. This is great news because you have the self- control to have pure thoughts, a pure heart, and pure motives, going forward. Everything you have endured thus far has attempted to rob you of your destiny by weighing heavily on your heart and emotions. When you identify who the real enemy is, then you can strategize to overcome and control impure thoughts and actions. Many become defeated because they have been fighting their own battles and not surrendering them to God. When you become tired and defeated, it is easier to give into your addictions.

David was a shepherd boy, and while he was tending to the sheep he was chosen as King, even after his brothers testified that he was the youngest and not fit for the position. He was selected because of his heart and not because of his popularity.

Queen Esther was an orphan, and she won favour with the Persian King because of her heart to save the Jewish nation and not just because of her beauty. She called a three day fast as part of her assignment, and consecrated herself to see the promise fulfilled. What are you prepared to do to get God's attention? Are you no longer content with what the world has to offer? God wants you to seek Him more intimately and to pursue Him.

It takes a 'great spiritual awakening' after a global pandemic to search for answers from within and realise that the Giver of life knew everything all along. It was a setup for your gain!

Take a moment to stop wherever you are and take hold of where you want to be. There is an end goal in the invisible that is yet to manifest. Now think of reasons for how you will get and stay there. You cannot go forward if you don't know where to start. Many fail because they do not have a plan for their life. You do not have to be one of them. Your identity is found in Him.

As long as the enemy keeps you in shame and condemnation you will not see your destiny. Change your perspective and stay in the cave of preparation until it's time to come out. Get rid of all the negative voices in your surroundings and use the lifeline God has given you to be the best you can be. May thankfulness and gratitude be the meditation of your heart, in remembrance of how far you have come against all the odds.

Spiritual Nutrients and Contaminants

One of the most powerful means towards spiritual purity is the control of our thoughts and words. The things we meditate on in our hearts dictate our words and actions. Thoughts have a way of coming out of our mouths and can be a blessing or a curse to ourselves or to others. If you want to know why your speech is impure, find out what you were thinking about and you will locate the root cause.

One attitude that can defile your spiritual purity is jealousy. If your heart is filled with jealousy, everything you do flows from there. Jealousy is a secret sin of the heart. It is an attitude that feeds strife and anger, and it brings division.

Meet Jessica. She is a beauty therapist and suffers from low self-esteem. She recently completed her studies and she loves volunteering at local soup kitchens in her community. She met her friend Katy at university and they have been friends ever since. Katy was very ambitious and started her own business and a non-profit organisation to mentor the youth. Jessica and Katy prayed and fellowshipped together on a regular basis and shared their future goals and dreams.

Jessica became envious of Katy's achievements because she did not fully comprehend who she herself was, and what she was born to do. In the past she had lost her car and had failed at following through with a business idea. The jealousy was subtle at first, but the more she thought about Katy's achievements, the more the 'green-eyed monster' reared its ugly head. In her heart she carried resentment towards her friend because she had not dealt with her own underlying issues. She started isolating herself and found excuses not to attend any of Katy's events. Her pride got the better of her and she now finds herself in a place of finding fault in every relationship.

It is a sad reality that many are caught in the trap of this particular spiritual contaminant. We should continually check our hearts lest we fall prey to jealousy and envy. Do we recognise and appreciate the value of others' gifts? And do we celebrate others' victories? When we speak is it wholesome or destructive talk? If we do not humble ourselves to admit that our perceptions may be wrong, we will never be content with who and where we are. Our reasoning will come from impure motives. Comparison kills our joy. Knowing and understanding our identity is essential to becoming spiritually and sexually pure.

Should a parent wait until their children are a certain age to discuss the consequences of pre-marital sex and its harsh realities, or allow them to discover it for themselves? Your children will never have to go through what you are struggling with if you address the issues openly with them now. Parents should also provide a biblical pattern for their children, as a married couple. Children learn more from what they see than what they hear.

Godly patterns

Your earthly father is your first love. He is supposed to take you on your first date and show you how to be loved. He is supposed to model how you ought to be treated. We need earthly fathers to be whole so that when we go out into the world, we know what to look for in a man. I was already married when I decided to take my dad out for lunch and go on 'our first date' as father and daughter to spend some time together. I was not going to hold my breath and wait for him to do it, so I initiated the moment. I explained to him the reason for the drive and the importance of the relationship between father and daughter. He just smiled and stared at me with approval for the idea. It was a beautiful, sunny day and the beach was walking distance from where we enjoyed our meal. We talked, laughed, shared stories, and savoured spontaneous moments that created memories that I will treasure in my heart forever.

The enemy has a counterfeit for the 'first love' relationship between father and daughter. When a younger woman dates an older man with benefits they call the man a 'sugar daddy'. This, in itself, is morally twisted. It is not a coincidence that there is a play on words in this expression, and that the word 'daddy' is used as indicating some form of satisfaction. No woman should ever feel that she needs to exchange her body for gifts and sensual pleasures. This is a practice that will result ultimately in rejection. If our relationships are unhealthy, our communities will be unhealthy too. Our children are in need of mentors and father figures who will restore their trust and dignity and exemplify love to them.

Take heart and be of good cheer however, if your earthly father lacked, faulted, or was absent. Your Heavenly Father is, and always was, present, and He completed and sealed your destiny with a promise to be with you always and to have your best interests at heart.

Courting and Dating

When your parents meet your friends for the first time, there has to be an uncomfortable conversation of what lies ahead in terms of the relationships. If you are a young adolescent and decide to 'court' someone, this is somewhat different from what the world refers to as dating. The difference between the two is that a courting couple intends to become engaged or married, and a dating couple may not have any specific expectations for the relationship. Dating means that you're just having fun and leaving to chance where the relationship goes, figuring it out along the way. This leads to unmet expectations and both parties getting hurt in the process.

Courting should be pursued in such a way that sexual purity is maintained as the norm. If you are a man, be intentional about protecting and safeguarding a woman's purity. You are your sister's keeper and have a moral responsibility towards her in pursuit of sexual purity, whether she will be your future spouse or not. The consequences of defiling your bodies are detrimental towards your emotional state of mind, and they affect your quality of life in the long term if wrong choices are made. Sex is a beautiful gift from God. You both owe it to your future spouse to wait before indulging in sensual pleasures, and to unveil this gift in the protective environment of the marital covenant. If he/she is not willing to wait until marriage, it should be a deal breaker. Infatuation or lust rushes. True love waits.

If you as a woman have endured rape, sexual abuse, and/or incest, you have the ability to control your future by pursuing purity again and choosing wholeness and a lifestyle of being the victor, not the victim. No one can imagine the pain you had to endure, but what I do know, is that you can use it as your weapon to set others free. Purity can still be pursued after making a commitment to honour God.

God spoke to me while I was enslaved in sexual impurity. He whispered that He has something better for me. It was as if I was in a slumber and oblivious to the bondage that the lusts of the flesh had me in. I did not even consider the dire consequences that awaited until after I made the decision to honour God. He called me out of promiscuity into a lifestyle of purity and I have never turned back. Purity flows from knowing you are loved and accepted by God, regardless of your past mistakes. When the focus is on Christ and obedience to Him, you do not have to struggle with temptations. He already prepared a way out before you were even tempted.

Before You Say "I Do"

Let me start by saying that singleness is not a curse! Singleness is about loving, valuing, and accepting yourself before sharing yourself with someone else. We don't go into a relationship seeking these elements but to add value to what's already birthed in us. This sets an environment to cultivate healthy relationships. It comes from a place of being whole and knowing who you are. Your partner would then reciprocate by loving you after dealing with issues of his or her past. This embodies a Christ-like relationship.

Being married or having children does not complete you, add to your identity, or necessarily add anything to your destiny. God can still use you in the midst of your singleness. You are complete in every season because God has already validated you. If you do decide to get married one day, let it be for the right reasons. If you are a woman in pursuit of marriage, never look to another man to love you more than you are capable of loving yourself. The covenant of marriage needs you whole. Everyone considers themselves an expert in giving marriage advice, often especially your friends who are not married. Their intentions may be good, however, it's best to consult God when faced with challenges because every marriage is different. The hardest thing for me was to let go of being independent. Life was no longer about me but about us. God had to work on me. He moulded and refined me.

Marriage is a perfect and Godly institution between two imperfect people. However, it won't numb your loneliness, get rid of your emotional baggage, or remove the ungodly soul ties. Be sure to become healed and restored before you give yourself to your future spouse. Love only takes you to the altar. Do not be swept away by the worldly view that holds onto the possibility of a marriage ending in divorce. The bad experience of others does not have to dictate the choices you make. Your ability to be dedicated and committed, respect one another, sacrifice for one another, and openly communicate with each other, will be what knits you together. Honesty is non-negotiable.

Commit to pray for your future spouse and that any emotional baggage will be resolved. Marriage is self-less and requires you to reflect God in how well you serve one another, and to cover and pray for each other every day. It is so much more than being loved and your individual needs being met. Pre-marital counselling lays the foundation for your individual expectations to be voiced and exchanged, and helps you to understand and prepare for the synchronising of your dreams and goals before you say "I do". Pre-marital counselling saved our marriage before it even began. David and I were honest about our expectations and wrote them down. We went through our list of expectations together and identified the deal breakers, which were things we were not willing to compromise. If you fail to do that, you set yourself up for surprises in marriage a few years down the line. A Christ-like marriage is more than the vows that you are exchanging. To love one another as Christ has commanded us is not easy, but it is worth it. I would do it all over again!

Spiritual preparation is key before the actual wedding takes place. It would be a tragedy to discover, one year into marriage, that you do not want the same things. Make your intentions clear from the word go. Your relationship becomes a three-fold cord which is not easily broken when God takes first place in your love triangle. It will cost you, but you will need to forgive quickly, and to reject any flaws that try to creep into your relationship.

As you become one, there will be some arguments you will have to lose in order to be able to win in the relationship. It is not about who is right, but who is willing to soften his or her heart and stay humble. Offense can lead to anger, which can turn into bitterness and give birth to strife. God has a purpose for uniting two imperfect beings and connecting them with destiny to address a need in society. Don't rush into love for the sake of time running out. God has a divine date which is never late. Your manual is found in the written word of God, and being in agreement is your weapon against the wiles of the enemy. Where there is unity, our Heavenly Father commands a blessing.

Two individuals from different backgrounds, experiences, beliefs and values are being joined together to create their own mosaic. The covenant of marriage teaches you to look into the mirror and first fix what is wrong with yourself before finding fault in your future spouse. Do not compete with one another; rather complement each other. Your journey of growth demands that you embrace the fact that you will not be the same individuals five years after exchanging your vows; you grow into your unique identity. When you face a crisis in your relationship, you need to adapt and overcome the challenges that may come. Financial strain is one of the biggest burdens in a marriage, so be sure to address this at the beginning with the utmost transparency.

Future wives and husbands, submission is not a death sentence or there to punish you. In fact, when you submit to God first, it enables you to be led by your future spouse. Many couples have a misinterpretation of biblical submission because of the examples of marriage they had in growing up. You have to receive God's Agape love first before you can love your future spouse unconditionally. If the source of your affection and compassion is contaminated, the chances are that you will base love on how you feel, when, in fact, love is a choice you have to make daily. It is a privilege to work towards a common goal in a Christ-like relationship and to be an expression of who God is, in the earth. I find great joy in dreaming, planning, growing, and exploring, and having someone that I am accountable to. Our passions and spiritual connection increase our intimacy in love, without any fence around our hearts. David is my best friend and the protector of my heart. He covers me when I am overwhelmed by my emotions, and when my dreams are bigger than me. I pray for him to fully embrace who he is destined to be. Two are better than one.

PART 2

MY LOVE STORY WITH GOD

Chapter Five

REDEEMING LOVE

For I am convinced that neither death nor life, neither angels nor demons, neither the present nor the future, nor any powers, neither height nor depth, nor anything else in all creation, will be able to separate us from the love of God that is in Christ Jesus our Lord.
(Romans 9:38-39, NIV)

Rebirth

My defining moment came when I was invited to a social gathering at Lira's place. I was staring into blank space surrounded by people all around me. Something was happening to me. This was not the life I wanted. There was a greater purpose for my life and I knew it. This was not me. It was who I pretended to be!!

My cravings for drinking and smoking just disappeared after that night. This occurred a few months before I was redeemed by God's love. I believe that these events leading up to my experience were divine appointments. I was experiencing an awakening, and as a result I wanted more for my life.

It was 30 March 2013, during Passover on Resurrection Sunday, when I received Jesus Christ as my Lord and Saviour and my journey to purpose and destiny began. A few days before encountering God in my living room, my colleague, Melissa, collapsed in the parking lot at work and passed away shortly afterwards. Two of my colleagues at work said she had meningitis, and friends who were close to her did not disclose any details concerning her condition. She was a born again believer, and those who knew her described her as a warrior woman of faith and prayer who was unashamed of the gospel. The moment I received the news of her death it was as if a veil was lifted from my eyes, and my heart flooded with gratitude that I was still breathing and that God's hand was over me. I had found a new appreciation for life. God is always speaking even when we choose to follow our own desires and are not plugged in to Him to be able to hear His voice clearly.

God wanted my attention. A Joyce Meyer encouragement clip I was watching spoke directly to me. I knew about God but had no personal relationship with Him. I messaged my friend Chanel and told her that I wanted to give my life to Jesus. She shared the 'sinner's prayer' with me. As I confessed it out loud, I expected to hear a sound of some sort or to feel something. I experienced none of that. What had I been thinking? Where I got the notion that it was supposed to happen a certain way was beyond me. It was probably an innate response to the false beliefs I had held unto. However, as I prayed, I felt a burden lift off my shoulders, an indescribable peace filled me, and I wept in the presence of God. I had found the missing piece of my puzzle, and I had started living again, instead of existing.

I phoned my mother after my divine encounter that Sunday. As soon as she picked up I could hardly contain myself and told her, "Guess what happened?" She asked me if I had won the lotto or met Joyce Meyer, knowing that I had bought all her books. I replied, "No mom." There was a silence at the other end of the line waiting in anticipation for my answer. I eventually said "Something way better than that: I gave my life to the Lord." It is not a coincidence that it's referred to as 'spreading the good news of the gospel' because you want to tell everyone about it.

At the same hour, minute and second my husband (boyfriend at the time) accepted Jesus as Lord over his life in Mozambique, where he was working as a remote paramedic. I still remember the excitement in his voice; he could not wait to share the news with me telephonically. We both relived our intimate moment with God and anticipated our reunion and future together.

A couple of days after our conversation David fell ill and collapsed at the campsite in Mozambique. One of his colleagues transported him to a local hospital which was a few kilometres away from their base, then contacted me to let me know. My heart sank immediately, but my first reaction was to start a prayer chain to petition to God to save his life. God gave me three confirmations that night and I knew deep inside that God would not give us a glimpse of our future and then bring us this far to let him die without fulfilling his purpose.

The doctor suspected meningitis and David was airlifted to Johannesburg for further tests and treatments. At the hospital in Johannesburg the doctor monitored him for a few days, but all the tests came back negative. Our prayers had been answered! He was discharged from hospital and flew back to Cape Town where I met him upon arrival.

After David's narrow escape from death, he had, unbeknown to me, decided to surprise me upon landing in Cape Town. He had to leave all his belongings behind in Mozambique because of his emergency evacuation, and was left with only the clothes on his back. He convinced me that he should buy a few things that we needed for a one night stay at the Crystal Towers Hotel; this stay was supposedly offered by his employers after his medical emergency in Mozambique. Prior to checking in, we enjoyed lunch in Blouberg Strand at one of our favourite spots, and then he said he had to slip away to run an errand. His behaviour made me suspicious and I had a feeling that he had something up his sleeve that day.

We headed towards the hotel at an alarmingly slow speed, but, for some reason, the rooms were not ready yet. The sweat was literally dripping from his face, and he stepped out to get some fresh air. About half an hour later we were escorted down a passage and stood in front of the door, as the manager swiped the key to open it.

As we entered the room, we were greeted by rose petals scattered on the bed, handmade towel-swans, and a small box on the counter. David had it all figured out and appeared nervous for what was about to take place. He kneeled down and after removing the ring from the box, placed it on the wrong finger! I had a good giggle. David had secretly been planning all this during his time away in Mozambique.

Savouring our special moment, we immediately announced the great news to our family and friends. Later, we spent the night in the superior luxurious room, but, in spite of all the frills in the room and the romantic ambience setting the mood, we decided to honour God from that moment on by waiting until we could say "I do". Another chapter had been birthed for us as a couple, although we were oblivious to what God wanted to do in and through our lives.

God ordained our steps in the ensuing weeks. My friend Bernie invited us to a 'victory weekend' and we were baptised as a couple. We grew closer as God moulded and refined us into who He wanted us to be.

David is from a small town named Humansdorp, in the Eastern Cape and what attracted me to him was his sense of adventure and the strides he takes when he walks. He bungee jumped more than 200 times while he was working at the canyon at Oribi gorge in southern KwaZulu-Natal. The most adventurous activity I ever did was a tree top canopy tour at Storms River Adventures, where I explored the unequalled beauty of the indigenous forest high up on ten treetop platforms, ziplining from one to the next. I later discovered that David had helped build the zipline of the exact canopy tour I braved in 2003, during his adventure guiding days, before I even met him. I thought that surely God found humour in how we ended up being together. I would have to dust off my bucket list and get back in the game. David had an intriguing résumé: scuba diver, adventure guide, skipper, fisherman, rock climber, abseiling specialist, rescue diver and life guard in Dubai.

At this time I had to make sure of what I was getting myself into with David by doing a thorough assessment. After all my toxic dating experiences, I was cautious. David must have seen something in me when he decided to stay behind in the city pursuing this girl with her bubbly personality. Well, if he had only known the emotional baggage that came along with it, and that God was going to use him to soften my heart! We came from different backgrounds and beliefs. A changed perspective leads to a renewed life and I was challenged to view the world through a different lens by being intentional about evolving into who I was destined to be.

David and I were married seven months after his initial proposal, and we grew spiritually with the guidance of spiritual mentors, Godly counsel, and continual fervent prayers. Our pre-marital counselling was facilitated through a God-fearing pastoral couple, and this laid a solid foundation for the covenant we were entering into. We had a renewed love for God and for our families and friends. We were determined to pursue God and to submit our lives to Him in every way. God's love kept us on track.

David resigned from being a flight paramedic in 2018 and decided to start his own business so he could live a purposeful life and build a legacy. It has been an honour serving alongside him and living out our calling as a married couple. He is a story teller with a wonderful sense of humour that will leave you in stitches. He has a strong character with a compassion for the lost. He is a man after God's own heart.

The Transforming Love of God

God's unconditional love (agape love) forms the basis of our transformations and breakthroughs. Any trials we face serve a purpose. His love is unmatched and no one – neither husband nor wives or anyone on earthcan compare to it. John 3:16 gave this account of it: *For God so [greatly] loved and dearly prized the world, that He [even] gave His [One and] only begotten Son, so that whoever believes and trusts in Him [as Saviour] shall not perish, but have eternal life.*

The first time I experienced accelerated spiritual growth was in my marriage. Our sowing, giving, and tithing was the foundation of God transforming us. Sowing is a spiritual law that gives God permission to act on our behalf. Tithing is more than just giving to God, it disciplines us to be faithful and good stewards of the resources He bestows on us. Giving is an act of worship. The reverential fear of the Lord is the beginning of wisdom and everything we do is to please Him and obey His commands. We plan our mornings as a couple at midnight, and invest time in our prayer life as our devotion to God. It should not be motivated by a religious act, ritual, or based on our performance, but from a place of worship rendered unto God. When we seek His righteousness, He gives us His abundance. We should seek His presence, not only His presents.

David and I entered every new season together, we slayed spiritual giants together, went through the valley and sang praises on the mountain tops as a union. We renewed our minds daily with the word of God, and submitted ourselves to Him. We lived to spend time in the secret place of His presence. God restored and redeemed us for a greater purpose; He transformed our spiritual DNA when He chose us as His vessels. We exchanged our old, filthy rags for His cloak of righteousness. The former things had passed away and the new things had come. We were a new creation. God kept us for a kingdom assignment. To be apostolic and prophetic leaders in this generation, was all part of His plan. If He can do it for us, He can do it for you. We have not arrived where we want to be, but thank God we are not where we use to be. His strength is made perfect in our weaknesses. We are also not oblivious to the fact that, as ministers of God's word, we are not exempted from sexual sin, hence we need to remain accountable to our spiritual covering and to one another.

God's love is what forms the foundation for genuine God-honouring love for one another in our lives. Love is a choice and not a feeling. Sacrificial love is laying down our lives, our will, and our desires in order to follow His will for our lives. We are all created by God in His image, but cannot all claim to be children of God unless we are saved and adopted into His kingdom through repentance of our sins and acceptance of Him as Lord of our lives.

This is not about religion but about having a personal living relationship with Jesus Christ. The greatest commandment is written in Matthew 22:37- 39 which says, *Love the Lord your God with all your heart and with all your soul and with all your mind. This is the first and greatest commandment. And the second is like it. Love your neighbour as yourself.*

God does not love us because we are good, He loves us because He is good. The love of God has a way of penetrating to the depths of our souls and spirits (inner man). We have all been designed with the desire to know God whether we recognise it or not, and only He can fulfil that desire. There is always the 'something missing' outside of receiving His redemptive love. We may try to fill this void with the things of this world, or with all forms of substances, sex, or temporary other satisfactions, but these simply leave us emptier than ever. Many broken men and women have had no example of what love should look like. The enemy uses this to open the door to lust and pervert God's intended plan for our lives. He sets a trap through offense, anger, bitterness, and strife to keep us in bondage. We can either allow our pain to alert us to our need, and allow God to heal us, or we can remain bitter and isolate ourselves from the rest of the world.

Through it all, God has a plan for our lives which He predestined and foreordained before the foundations of the earth were even formed.

Whether you have been adopted, orphaned, abandoned, abused, or rejected by loved ones, know that you are loved and accepted by a good Father who wants to make you whole. He will never leave you nor forsake you. He is not a man that He should lie. He never disappoints. Our Heavenly Father is a God of restoration whose grace and mercies are new every day. His unconditional love is what saves us from darkness, suicidal thoughts, rejection, unworthiness, and addictions.

There is no fear in Love, but perfect loves drives out all fear, because fear has to do with punishment. The one who fears is not made perfect in love. (1 John 4:18, NIV)

When you pursue God with your whole heart, He shows up in ways unimaginable to the human mind and heart. There is no sin too great and nothing you confess that can stop God from loving you. It is unexplainable although everyone experiences Him differently. His nature is one of complete faithfulness without being a respecter of persons. His promises are "Yes" and "Amen" to every believer, and He is the same God yesterday, today, and forevermore, who never changes.

If you are reading this and you are struggling with rejection, receive God's unconditional love. You do not have to allow anger and condemnation to rule your life any longer. There is power in a made-up mind. Although it is a process to be healed from ungodly soul ties and soul wounds, you are one step closer to your destiny when you take the decision to accept God's love. You are fearfully and wonderfully made, and loved by your Creator, not for what you do on an everyday basis, but for who He is. God is Love. When you learn and accept that your identity is not found in your occupation, the car you drive, or the amount of money in your bank account, but in who your Heavenly Father made you to be, you start to see that He is a good Father who has forgiven you and given you a unique identity in Christ and an assignment to fulfil on this earth. Let that sink in.......

Forgiveness

Forgiveness is the key to freedom. When we experience God's forgiveness toward us, it sets us completely free from guilt and shame toward Him, and it puts us on a path of being able to forgive others. We forgive because God forgave us first. The moment we forgive those who have hurt or offended us, our journey of wholeness can begin. It is important to recognise that one of the greatest hindrances to our faith is unforgiveness. Unforgiveness keeps us in bondage and prevents our prayers from being answered. We need to deal with every disappointment, every regret, every past mistake, and most importantly, we need to learn to forgive ourselves. It is an act of faith, and completely necessary if we want God to promote us to the next season of possibilities. Forgiveness is not about the other person, but about letting go of the offense, even if the other person was wrong. If we don't forgive, we become prisoners, enslaved by our own thoughts while the other person lives freely.

Unforgiveness may also be passed down a family line. It may originate from a particular offense and then evolve into strife when left unresolved and not dealt with. Unforgiveness can then feed a cycle of hurt, brokenness, and iniquity (a wicked act or thing) in our bloodline that can persist for four generations. One can describe it as a generational curse.

Generational Legacy

We become what we are exposed to. We learn certain behaviours and imitate words that are spoken while we are growing up. Generations have often been robbed through living a life of secrecy, where children simply accepted things the way they were for decades, never digging deeper to the root of the problem. The family dynamics are left broken with no direction from the father figure due to a lack of submission to God. The enemy's tactic is to destroy families so that they never function in the healthy way God intended for them. Don't get caught up fighting demons your forefathers neglected to deal with. May you be the first generation to break the generational curse over your family.

Many destinies have been aborted because generations failed to pass sustainable legacies on to their children to enable them to chase their dreams and pursue their purpose. Many such families merely existed, and learned to survive, instead of thriving and living out their God-ordained purpose. In this next generation, the power of love can tear down the veil of fear and open up a world of endless possibilities.

God searches our hearts and rewards our obedience to forgive and to be led by the Holy Spirit instead of by our emotions. This requires a mere mustard seed sized faith and trust in God. When you have destiny in mind, it determines your behaviour and how you spend your time, focus, and energy. Emotions are fickle and changeable, but the word of God and its power to transform remain the same, and they are eternal.

We are only able to forgive if we internalise then live out the true meaning of love: *Love is patient, love is kind. It does not envy, it does not boast, it is not proud. It does not dishonour others, it is not self-seeking, it is not easily angered, it keeps no record of wrongs. Love does not delight in evil but rejoices with the truth. It always protects, always trusts, always hopes, always perseveres. Love never fails.* (1 Corinthians 13:4-8, AMP)

Honour Your Parents

Honour [esteem, value as precious] your Father and your Mother [and be respectful to them]-this is the first commandment with a promise – so that it may be well with you, and that you may have a long life on earth. (Ephesians 6:2, AMP)

There is a reward attached to respecting your parents regardless of how you were treated. There is no exception to the promises of God. If you became a victim of your circumstances, all you can do is strive to do better, but when you open your heart to God's unconditional love, you are empowered to break generational curses over your life and the lives of your family. However, it is vital to maintain a soft heart in the process. Hardheartedness is a breeding ground for pride, and will not achieve anything constructive. It requires humility to lay new foundations for living an abundant life, and requires both humility and honour for the exercise of true godly spiritual authority in a spirit of love.

A spirit of rebellion does not please God, so fathers also should be careful not to provoke anger in their children. If we are advocating for restoration in families, we need to accept the responsibility from both sides of the coin. God never changes His word to suit us. He commands us to remain under His covering while He is working things out for our good.

Love requires us to be truthful without any hidden agendas; God searches our motives. A person in error will have to give an account for every word spoken and action taken. We need to stop blaming our parents and admit our own faults if we want to see a love revolution in this generation. If you have never told your parents how much they mean to you, it is a good time to do it now. If you have resentment towards your mother or father, it is the right time to pick up the phone and ask for forgiveness, even if they were in the wrong. When there is no reason to love them, love them anyway. Love covers a multitude of sins and it starts with you. You only have the ability to change your own reactions and area of influence. God honours relationships, so we must be good stewards of the ones God has bestowed on us. If God had a plan for you to belong to another family, He would have orchestrated it that way. You need to honour those whom He, in His wisdom, decided should be your parents.

Many have no opportunity to exercise this principle as they have lost both their parents, but honour may still be exercised through our attitudes and words regarding them. Honour is never about the person but having a submitted heart towards God.

If you follow God's will, He will pay the bill.

Passing It On

Children are a blessing from God, whether they have been conceived in or out of wedlock. Sarah gave birth to Isaac in her old age and Hagar, an ancient Egyptian servant, gave birth to Ishmael. Both of them came from the seed of Abraham, yet Ishmael was conceived with a servant who was not his wife. Abraham and Sarah were not prepared to wait for God to bless them. God's time is not our time. God stayed true to His promise and told Abraham's wife Sarah that at an appointed time she would give birth to the promised son, Isaac. Ishmael received the blessing, but Isaac got the inheritance. Many times we plan and implement a future that is not part of God's plan and destiny for us, because we are impatient, frustrated, and lack wisdom. This may have lasting negative effects. To this day Ishmael and Isaac are in conflict in the Middle East.

If you love a child, you will not enable his or her addiction, and you will not feed the broken paradigm. The rage and anger that many millennials are experiencing has caused a barrier to restoration in families, which in turn leads to repetitive cycles of anger and brokenness. It is necessary to get to the root of the anger, and deal with the lingering issues. They will not merely go away. You have to decide to break the generational cycles in your family line.

Many parents today are praying for their children to be set free from drug addiction, alcohol abuse, and gang violence. Ephesians 4:26 states that we can *Be angry [at sin-at immorality, at injustice, at ungodly behaviour], yet do not sin; do not let your anger [cause you shame, nor allow it to] last until the sun goes down.* God's view of healthy families is very different from the worldly view, which is the enemy's deceptive perversion of the original design.

Every time an aircraft takes flight there is a possibility that a decompression may occur. A decompression is a sudden loss or gradual decrease of cabin pressure. When the oxygen masks fall down, you first have to place the mask over your own nose and mouth before you put it on someone else. If you are not ok, the person next to you will not be ok. After pulling the mask down, you have to fasten your seatbelt and breathe normally. The same principle applies to life. Before you invest in anyone else, you have to value yourself. If you are secure, your children become secure and whole. When you receive your inner healing, and exchange your pain for the love of God, it becomes a setup for miracles to happen in your children's lives. You will have to lead the way for your children if you want them to imitate you and become agents of change in society.

Passing It On In Our Society

We need to create platforms in educational institutions, churches, virtual online platforms with millennials, youth workshops, schools, libraries and households that will spread awareness of the social advantages of building, healthy families, and promote efforts towards achieving this. God instituted the covenant of marriage and the design of families that would bring glory to His name, before the fall of man. The enemy's plans are to steal, kill, and destroy in order to pervert God's master design. The reason that our youth is perishing is because they have not been given the tools for restoration in the correct setting. It is everyone's responsibility to impart Godly principles into our youth and future leaders. If you have daughters, you need to set boundaries in place to protect her from mistaking lust for love. Is the church doing enough to address these addictions? Are ministers of God preaching the consequences of pre-marital sex, and sharing on how to find a root to the problem, or have we turned a blind eye? Change starts with us.

Chapter Six

CHANGING SEASONS

For every thing there is a season, and a time to every purpose under the heaven. (Ecclesiastes 3:1, KJV)

Nothing is permanent except God and His promises. Everything you go through is only for a season; it doesn't last. Seasons give us hope for what is next. Seasons remind us that change is inevitable and they prompt us to relook our perspectives. There is a close relationship between seasons and the different stages in the life of an individual. There is a time to weep, a time to mourn, a time to plant, and a time to laugh in every season. God blesses you in seasons and you bear fruit in seasons. What you perceive as being buried, God sees as being planted in a particular season, to grow you. It may not feel like you are entering a new season, but, just like the branches of a tree go through a pruning stage when seasons change, your circumstances have to change.

In order to paint a picture of the road to destiny, I will be sharing personal experiences of transition that will illustrate the transformational power of discerning the seasons. During trying times, if you don't confront certain things, you don't overcome them, and you run the risk of becoming stagnant and being stuck in an old season. Transition is a transformation from the inside out. It is the hardest thing to be still and wait on God, when everything inside of you wants to move. This posture requires you to be focused. If you are being tested, you are possibly in a transition.

For twenty seven years while living in Bonteheuwel I attended a local church, but there was no spiritual growth in my life. The only reason I attended this church was because it was tradition in our family to be in church on a Sunday. I experienced no true expression or evidence of the Holy Spirit. I religiously went to church, but I was spiritually dead. I started attending church less frequently than I used to. Something was missing! I knew about God but there was no relationship.

My friend Bernie invited us to her church seven years ago, after David and I had our divine encounter with God and made a covenant with Him in marriage. We rented an apartment in the northern suburbs and visited the church for a year before committing to be 'covenant members'. We met with our life group every Thursday evening and shared the word of God through fellowship, encouragement, and prayer. After a few years, our regional leaders equipped and empowered us to facilitate the life group. The spiritual growth we experienced during this season unlocked the potential God placed within us. Deep down we felt a conviction that God had buried us like a seed in the ground, and would ultimately shift us into our next season. God is not confined to our time, and He works in seasons. When we refer to days or seasons, we are not referring to actual time on a clock or calendar; we are referring to the timing of the Lord. God's timing is not our timing.

We sat down with our senior pastor and shared what we felt the Lord wanted us to do. David and I agreed that we would not function in a position God had not called us to, and that we would wait for the right platform. Our hidden potential and higher calling is not always visible to the naked eye, and leaders will often point out where they think you should serve within a ministry. It was a back and forth for two years before David and I were released, after serving at the church for six years, to begin our journey of trusting God where we could not see. At this moment we knew that God had given us gifts to equip the church, but the environment was not conducive. The timing and sequence were pivotal. The substance of our character, while in the wilderness, was more important than the actual gifts we were carrying. As a kingdom citizen you are not abandoning God if you leave your local church; this view is a religious mindset that needs to be uprooted. You do not alienate yourself from individuals who are not a part of your church or denomination. This is not Christ-like behaviour. God does not call us to a denomination; He calls us to the Kingdom of God for a specific audience, with a specific message for His people.

Transitioning

We were mentored and spiritually reared by Ps Chana Richards whom we met four years ago during a time of transition and God established the foundation for the works of ministry He was preparing us for. Ps Chana is a former teacher, and has an apostolic grace to position her students into alignment with God's purpose. She has been a tremendous blessing in our life as a ministry couple. After much conviction in our hearts, fasting and prayer, hearing God's voice and Godly counsel, we stepped out in faith, and we were ordained as pastors. We joined a community church we had visited before (with missionaries from the United Kingdom), and served as associate pastors for a year before our season ended during the global pandemic in 2019.

Our season at the community church was part of our assignment. We had been positioned to serve people, not a building, with our God-given gifts, and so our focus was the people God called us to, and the gifts that He wanted to stir up in us and develop, to serve them. I never envisioned being called to ministry in a million years, but God chooses us, we don't choose Him! I learned that God qualifies the called; He does not necessarily call the qualified. He never chooses you based on your qualifications, but based on your availability to do His work, and on your heart to serve His people. *Many are the plans in a person's heart, but it is the Lord's purpose that prevails.* (Proverbs 19:21, NIV)

After our release at the community church, we entered a season of 'pruning' and fully surrendering to the leading of the Holy Spirit.

God was ordering our steps and we followed. God re-aligned us into our respective offices as apostolic and prophetic leaders of this generation, and birthed our prophetic ministry. Our spiritual covering, Apostle Taswell and his wife, Prophetess Edwina, led the proceedings for the ordination and began walking a journey with us. We were assigned with destiny helpers to execute our heavenly mandate. God sometimes breaks something down, so He alone can rebuild it on a solid foundation. We are walking out the heart of God for His Church, which is the 'Bride of Christ'.

I believe that if we had not left our previous church the first time God spoke to us, we would have been stuck in an old season, but God pulled us closer to follow Him wholly. If you are finding yourself in a barren season, just know that help is on the way. God will never lead you to a place He does not first prepare you for. He is positioning you for your purpose! Frustration is a good sign that God is ready to promote you to a new season. Ask God to show you what He wants to teach you in every seasonal shift.

Every new season requires a deeper intimacy. Adopt an attitude of expectancy that you will steward with a fresh perspective, and be determined that you will follow in His footsteps without depending on the familiarity of the past season. This will bring new understanding and new revelation. God can only increase our capacity if we make room for more. We are ambassadors for Christ, coming up against the agents of darkness, with a Kingdom agenda to establish God's mandate on the earth and glorify Him.

We have to endure the process if we want to be all God has created us to be. Assess any cultural and religious beliefs that are contradictory to the word of God that may be keeping you in bondage at your current place of worship. These should be measured against what He wills for you. It is our obligation to align our will with God's will, and not to do things to obtain approval from man.

Seasonal Processes

There is a season to sow, a season to harvest, and a season to reap what you have sown over time. This is a spiritual law that God has given to promote His children to the next level. The harvest season is usually accompanied by a time of work, effort, and bearing much fruit. It is our job to make sure the seeds get planted, to water those seeds, and watch Him bring the harvest. If you don't work the soil, the seed falls on hard soil, and the harvest will not be plentiful.

David and I have endured seasons of persecution, rejection, slander, betrayal, and gossip against us because we had not served God for twenty years, or because we were not following a set religious programme. This is not a true reflection of followers of Christ, and the fruit these believers were displaying was a testament to the condition of their hearts. Spiritual maturity is measured by your level of obedience, not the number of years you have been saved. If you are young and gifted, and pressed on every side, God's grace is sufficient for you in this season. Do not be intimidated by religious folk, but pursue the call on your life.

It is our responsibility to know God on a personal level and to get an understanding of His character traits so that we do not become deceived by cultural paradigms about serving God. Deception removes something from you to deceive you. The enemy removes the truth and replaces it with a lie. In our case, this happened for our good, and it moulded us into resilient leaders. If we are followers of Christ, we submit to God first and should not be moved by people's opinions. We should stay focused on our kingdom assignments. You do not need anyone's permission to fulfil your purpose. If you have been hurt and disappointed in the church, seek Godly counsel from someone you trust and find healing of your soul wounds. You need to continue pursuing purpose while you are processing pain. What happened to you may not be your fault, but it is your responsibility to be healed from it. One can compare God's processing of our lives with a seed that is planted in good soil which will bear good fruit if the correct method is used for the tree to sprout, and the plant receives the proper nourishment. If the soil you are planted in is not fertile, it can frustrate the germination process, or the seed may die.

You were born with a multitude of seeds inside of you that need to be planted in the right soil, so that the flower can bloom. You cannot bloom where you have not been planted. Not everyone will understand your growth process and appreciate your unique beauty. God buries His treasures and uncovers them when He sees fit. If you do not identify the seasons, and more importantly when the seasons change, the seed within you may be choked, and this will delay or inhibit the growth process.

There are many people who have a relationship with God and are walking around with dormant gifts that the world needs. Perhaps the environment that you find yourself in is not conducive for the gifts to be developed. If you feel this may be the case with you, speak to your leaders about it, and share the fact that you are seeking God for direction. The last thing you want is to be in a ministry function God has not called you to. When you are at a crossroads, check your motive, even if it results in you making a mistake. God will move on your behalf when you have the right heart attitude. Stay clear of harbouring bitterness while in the waiting process. Are your leaders committed to your development and maturity? Are you equipped to step fully into the mandate God is calling you to?

Seasonal Assignments

At an appointed time, God places destiny helpers in your life to direct you to your next assignment. God promotes you based on the assignments that you complete. Your assignments are a build-up to your purpose, and they are also seasonal. The assignments may constantly change, and obedience is required to shift when God requires it of you. There is a rhythm and a timeline for every assignment from God. If you choose to ignore the voice of God, He will simply find someone else for the next assignment.

Your transformation is your responsibility. You will not know what is on the inside of you if you do not attempt to try something new, and to trust God to unveil His purpose for your life. Not everyone will embrace you, or understand how you are wired differently from others, when you move forward in pursuit of destiny. God spoke to you, not to them! God speaks to all of us individually, and one reason the next person may fail to understand your transitioning, is that they have not yet received the blueprint for their own life.

If you have become comfortable in this season and stuck in a place where you know your assignment has been completed, then there is a new season that is waiting for you which you have not yet transitioned to. You need to be prepared to move. You are not a tree! You need to separate your WHO from your DO.

New Mindset

As you transition with grace, you cannot take an old mindset or way of thinking into your future. The seed you are carrying might not bloom in a particular environment if there is a lack of nutrition and deprivation of oxygen. You may have all the required tools to grow, but the soil is not fertile. Not everyone is meant to nurture your seed. There needs to be an understanding about why it was planted in the first place. Therefore, the company you keep plays a vital role in your bearing fruit. If people can't feed you spiritual food to help you grow, you will be in the exact same place five years from now.

It is only through God's grace that David and I were saved together, baptised together, and ordained to be effective in the Kingdom as a couple. We are not fighting for a building; we are contending for the Body of Christ. We have been deployed to transmit a sound to the nations. As a young couple in ministry it can become daunting when your vision becomes bigger than you, but we have learned to trust God and embrace the call on our lives in every season. *It is not by might, nor by power, but My Spirit [of whom the oil is a symbol] says the Lord of hosts.* (Zechariah 4:6, AMP). God is pouring new wine into a new wineskin in this next season of our lives. There is an acceleration taking place in His Kingdom as He is positioning each vessel in its place, so that the promises of God can come to pass. If we are not relevant to the times we are living in, the chances are that we will lose sight of the prophetic move of God.

Chapter Seven

STAY IN YOUR LANE

For where jealousy and selfish ambition exist, there is disorder [unrest, rebellion] and every evil thing and morally degrading practice.(James 3:16, AMP)

Mind the Gap

I travelled to London for two weeks, accompanied by two research students, for the London 2012 Olympic Games, (an international multi-sport event), to collect data for a research project for my supervisor, Professor Kamilla Swart. The interviews were based on residents' perceptions of the safety aspects during the 2012 Olympics. The Underground Tube, which is a system of public transport consisting of trains that travel in tunnels below the city, was my transportation for the duration of my stay as we travelled between fan parks to interview both residents and supporters.

As I stepped into the Tube I would hear an audible voice saying, "Mind the gap". "Mind the gap" is an audible or visual warning phrase is- sued to rail passengers to have caution while crossing the horizontal, and in some cases vertical, spatial gap between the train door and the station platform. It is famous throughout the world as a catchphrase of the London Underground. The Tube managers discovered that an automated message made much more practical sense than station attendants and drivers warning and directing passengers all the time.

When we are at a detour, we can rely on the Holy Spirit to guide us into the right direction. If we take a wrong turn, we can rest assured that He will reroute us, because He has something waiting for us on the other side. God will never abandon us, and He is ready to catch us when we fall and make mistakes. It is interesting that the word used on the Tube system is to "mind" the gap; our usual practice is to react before thinking of our next move. We always need to be checking if we are on the right course, to process and perceive what lies ahead before continuing. When we are in the "gap" phase of our life, we have the option to stay where we are or take the leap of faith, listen to the voice, and jump into the moving train. Transition requires us to do things we have never done before

God will sound the alarm when we are heading in the wrong direction. He positions reinforcements in the form of people, challenges we face, and disruption, to give us a hint, and He will flag us down to change our course as soon as danger is approaching. May we always slow down and yield to the 'silent voice' during times of disruption in our lives.

Gifts and Talents are Signals

God wants us to desire spiritual gifts and He will give them to us to advance His Kingdom. My prayer to God as I grew up was always: Why am I here? God gives us hints along the way when He assigns people to us. These are divine appointments, so He can rescue us from our disobedience and lead us towards obedience to His call on our lives.

On the road to purpose you will discover that it is your talents and passions that cause you to grow and endure the trials. Every man or woman on the road to discovering who he or she is, discovers the unique creation that he or she is. All were born with a purpose and unique gifts. Their gifts are not for themselves; they are to set others free.

Fear of Men

One of the hindrances and challenges that we may encounter when we pursue destiny, is fear of others' opinions. This alters our beliefs and sets limitations on our capabilities. Most of the tests we will endure are related to the strongholds in our minds that define what it is to be successful. Have you ever talked yourself out of doing something, or talked yourself into an assignment that is not earmarked for you, because of fear and what people may think? You need to stay in the lane assigned to you, irrespective of people's opinions.

No assignment comes without its challenges. Your passion is your own unique heartbeat. When you are a born again believer, your mind does not become renewed automatically; you may remain stuck in religious beliefs. In my case I was younger than most of the women I was leading and empowering in the prayer groups I was overseeing, but there is no age in the spirit. You are promoted by God to the extent of your obedience. This is a kingdom principle that is yet to be grasped in its fullness when serving in ministry, but this is a topic for another book!

Remember to separate your WHO from your DO. If you do not know who you are, you will run in a lane never meant for you. The more you know God, the more your unique identity will be revealed. You have been called to solve a problem, to ignite purpose, or to bring a paradigm shift in the Kingdom of God through your gifts. Disruption in our lives is a reminder of the promise that awaits us.

Comparing Lanes

We must not get distracted by our challenges, shortcomings, or what others have to offer that we ourselves don't possess. When we compare our- selves with other women, we insult God. His original plan for mankind was that all should be uniquely designed. Jealousy and envy originate from our enemy, the father of lies, who plans and plots to steal, kill, and destroy lives. It is our responsibility to stay in our own lane, and to be the best version of ourselves that God created us to be. Focusing on another person's lane slows down our own momentum.

We were not designed to be in competition with, and envious of, one another. We are to encourage and sharpen each other. The enemy often uses the weapon of jealousy to cause division, strife, and discord among believers, in order to distract them from their own unique purposes, and prevent them from bearing any fruit. When other people are blessed before you, are you sincerely happy for them?

If you don't know the story of the woman in the race next to you, the chances are that you won't understand the glory of God on her life. There is no need to be jealous of someone else's 'coat' because God has one specifically for you.

Also, everyone's test is different. Where some fail at the first attempt to uproot their addiction, others get set free because they are desperate enough for change. You should never give up. Maintain a willingness to be set free, and be committed to change. There are thousands of people with testimonies that have not been heard. There are voices that have been silenced by the enemy, so that people remain imprisoned by their own thoughts. God is breaking the silence for a time such as this, so the captives can be set free from captivity, generational curses can be broken in family lines, and His dominion power can be manifested in the earth.

Obedience Helps You Stay the Course

We have been birthed to live, not just exist. God is waiting on our obedience to direct the next move. Obedience is the outward evidence of the fear of the Lord. The book of Hebrews also equates obedience with faith. If you believe that you can start a business, you will. If you believe that you can finish your studies, you can. The key focus is that you make a decision based on the power of a made-up mind. It is God's will for you to be healed from your brokenness and emotional wounds in order for Him to trust you with the next assignment.

When you succumb to soul wounds and look at life through the lens of disappointment and hurt, your destiny seems unreachable, but you need to remember that your perceptions are often coloured by broken filters and others' personal agendas that led to failure. God wants to change your perspective in order to change the course of your life. There is a purpose for every setback, dysfunctional relationship, disappointment, and rejection you have experienced. *And we know that in all things God work for the good of those who love him, who have been called according to his purpose. And those He predestined, He also called, He also justified; those He justified, He also glorified.* (Romans 8:28, 30, NIV)

The broken woman who is angry with every man she comes into con- tact with, and whom everyone is judging, is most likely bound by chains and needs your prayer. The woman who had an abortion and can't experience intimacy with her husband because of shame and guilt, needs your prayer. Or *you* might be that woman. If you are a man stuck in addictions, there is a way out if you follow the voice of your built-in God-given Purpose Strategist (GPS) – the Holy Spirit.

As flight crew we walked through different airports when flying into different countries. Upon my first visit to any country, the signage would seem blurry or I would miss the signs and directions. All the lanes looked similar, but only one led to the correct exit. Sometimes I found myself walking in circles after taking the wrong turn or exit, ultimately prolonging my journey. In the same way we can become lost in our lives and run in the wrong lane, while all the time the signs are there. We need to focus on what is ahead of us. The things that are unknown to you may be familiar to the person right next to you. Remember to keep going in your own lane, even if others seem to be making progress and you are not. When you step into the unfamiliar it is scary at first, but the choice is yours to have blind faith and trust God, or to remain stagnant. The excess baggage that you have carried for years cannot go with you to your next destination. We have all been given the power of choice but we are not exempted from the consequences and the direction we take.

Chapter Eight

THE SECRET PLACE

But when you pray, go into your most private room, close the door and pray to your Father who is in secret, and your Father who sees [what is done] in secret will reward you. And when you pray, do not use meaningless repetition as the Gentiles do, for they think they will be heard because of their many words. So do not be like them [praying as they do]; for your Father knows what you need before you ask Him.
(Matthew 6:6-8, AMP)

Prayer is the crux of our spiritual growth and the heartbeat of God. It is not a repetition of words to win favour with God. It is a simple heartfelt communication with God. Jesus went to the mountain of Gethsemane (olive- press), taking with Him Peter and the two sons of Zebedee, to commune with His Father and pray in secret before His betrayal and arrest. He went a little further from the disciples and pleaded three times for the coming hardships to be taken away. Jesus fell on His face, dying to Himself and His own will. The name of the mountain Jesus prayed at had great significance. It represented an olive-press. Olives are pressed hard and go through a crushing process to produce the best oil. There is a crushing that takes place on your way to purpose and the will of God. Jesus fulfilled His purpose on earth and His sacrificial love for us nailed Him on the cross. He died so that we could live.

There is power in prayer when you follow the example of Jesus Christ: going to His secret place, and praying in the early hours of the morning, while it was still dark. The midnight hour is the greatest time to effect change and transformation in the spiritual realm. By the time believers arise between 4 am and 6 am, the dark forces have completed their diabolical assignments. I am not saying that your prayers at any other time will be ineffective, just that the climate for breakthrough and declaration is set at the above prescribed times when you command your morning and order your day ahead.

What the enemy meant for harm when I was tempted at midnight as a young adolescent in our living room, God transformed into a divine battle plan to claim back territory for the kingdom. In hindsight, as my walk with God grew more intimate, He would wake me up between midnight and 3 am with divine impartations to enable me to execute His strategy in a ministry, business, and in my personal capacity. This prayer strategy produced results for me and it can potentially do the same for you if you are seeking fresh revelation. When I was travelling to different countries, I would adapt my prayer lifestyle to align to their time change. It is not about the time; it is the motivation behind it that counts.

Your silent prayers in secret will be rewarded publicly. There is a shift in the atmosphere when a God-fearing woman stands in the gap for her children. Many children caught up in rebellion have escaped death because of the righteous prayers of a woman wailing before God in the secret place. In this intimate relationship between you and God, God hears every word. Everyone has the ability to hear from God if they are plugged in to the right source, but not everyone becomes still enough to listen. Imagine wearing your headsets but not plugging it in to the outlet or device. The music is playing but you can't hear it. God is always speaking whether we hear Him or not. Doubt may creep in if you feel that your prayers have not been heard, but if you take time to plug in and listen, you will hear God speak in your heart, and this will enable you to discern the nature and timing of His answer.

The Holy Spirit reveals Jesus to us. Jesus is the answer to our every need. He forms part of the full Godhead which is Father, Son, and Holy Spirit. Before we are born again we are spiritually dead. There is only one way to the Father, and that is through His Son Jesus Christ who is the way, the truth, and the life.

The lusts of the flesh harden our hearts, and it becomes difficult to receive God's love and walk in humility. If you have led a lifestyle of secret sin, you will find that God knows everything, nothing is hidden from Him, and yet He is more than willing to deliver you. He extends to all the invitation to allow His help, and He then works from the inside (heart and soul) to the outside (your apparel and conduct). However, it is necessary to die to ourselves in order to become fully alive and tuned in spiritually.

When you are filled with the Holy Spirit, your heart is softened and prepared to hear from God. When you replace the noise with personal conversations with your Creator, you will experience true freedom. Constant boredom, and being continually faced with loneliness and temptations for superficial gratifications, are symptoms of living an unfulfilled life. Anger, unbelief, and double mindedness dissipate in the secret place of His presence as you spend more time there. This is the best place to work through inner battles and experience true worship with God. True worship is more than words that you sing. It is a lifestyle of thankfulness, honesty, obedience, and giving to those in need without expecting anything in return.

Seeking truth requires you to apologise to every person that you have hurt, and to release those who have offended you. Striving for a balanced life is necessary on your journey to wholeness. You become what you give the most attention to. Where do you spend most of your time? Have you invested in others more than yourself? Have you given up because of what life served you, or have you taken on the responsibility of helping others?

The moment has arrived to take your life back and discover your value. God has a unique blueprint with your name on it that no one can copy. You are still in the process of becoming the expression of that blueprint; do not be too hard on yourself. I have become resilient whenever I face trials, because my heartfelt prayer is not for God to remove the trial, but for Him to take me through it. I was transformed in this place, forgiven in this place, and gave up everything that was not aligned to God's purpose for my life in this place. The secret place is not where you make demands and transactions from God; it is where you get close to Him. It is where He restores you and brings you into His rest.

Prayer Journaling

Prayer journaling is one method of promoting inner healing. You can use it to write down your emotions, and to record God's answers to your prayers. It serves as a motivator: you can capture your dreams and goals for the future. Set time aside to take inventory of the areas in your life that are in a state of unrest. You can only get restoration if you identify the areas that need healing. Take a few deep breaths before starting. Get still in a quiet place and ask God a question by putting pen to paper. Wait a few minutes. You may get one word, a picture, or a statement. Pray and ask God to show you the places in your heart that need to be transformed. Write down some of the things that stood out during your time of silence. Give yourself permission to slow down and to acknowledge the areas that are out of balance. Remove any layers of false identity that you have held onto, and be as transparent as you can be. Another powerful reflection tool you can use is 'writing to heal'.

Writing-to-heal Tool

During the first four years of our marriage we struggled with sexual intimacy. I would get a random memory that would creep in at the most unexpected times, and I would just freeze. I thought something was wrong with me. I viewed sex as being dirty, and God had to renew my mind and heal my soul wounds. I had dealt with my ungodly soul ties, but some memories and vivid images still lingered in my mind. It was a constant battle. David was patient with me every single time. Inner healing is a process. You have to give yourself permission to heal. We cannot be 'super spiritual' and neglect to address the triggers of the soul. There is no need to suffer in silence. We can have emotions as long as they do not have us.

Writing is therapeutic, and it brings healing, especially if you find it difficult to express yourself or to talk about your past hurts. Acknowledge it if you are not okay. Write down the emotions, good or bad, that you are feeling. It will help you to give a language to your pain. It is also a method of transforming your stories of pain to stories of power. The idea is to dump your feelings on paper, not people. Decide to function no longer as a broken version of yourself. State your truth and where you find yourself right now. What feelings do you want to have in the future? You can only dominate your destiny if you are healed and have the freedom to be your AUTHENTIC SELF.

Select ONE pain point that you can commit to writing about (commit to 10 minutes a day). A pain point can be identified through the following indicators:

1. God and other people keep bringing this issue up to you.

2. This painful moment frequently affects your relationships with others.

3. You desperately want to be free in this area.

4. The audience that you are called to needs you to heal; the people that you serve will be negatively impacted if you do not become whole.

I believe this process will assist you in your journey to wholeness as you embrace your purpose. If you seek Him, you will find Him and hear His voice in the simplest way. He also speaks through people, books, your enemies, nature, and any vessel created by Him. Do not despise whom God uses to give you a life-altering message. He will use anyone to fulfil His purpose. Also every assignment has a time frame attached to it, so there is no time to waste.

Whatever you believe to be true is your reality. If you believe you will be stuck in addiction for the rest of your life, you will be stuck. When you make up your mind to change against all odds, you will change. The latter is the best choice you can make and it will shift the trajectory of your life for generations to come. The secret place mends your broken spirit and is a place of spiritual rest. It restores you so you can start hoping and dreaming again. It is the one place you can be wholly yourself and be set free.

Meet Barbara

When I first met Barbara she was an introvert and didn't know how to pray. She memorised the "Our Father" prayer of Jesus and struggled to communicate with God because of her past addictions and secret sins. She felt very uncomfortable about praying in front of others so she avoided it. She yearned for an intimate relationship with God, but she did not know where to start. A friend invited her to fellowship with a women's group where they spoke about the secret place. They then asked Barbara to pray. She froze. Her friend stepped up and prayed on her behalf. When she got home she went into her room and closed the door behind her. She wept and repented when the Lord spoke these word to her, "No amount of sin can change my mind about you. You have been forgiven a long time ago. My grace is sufficient for you." From that day onwards she became intentional about spending time in the presence of God. Barbara got her confidence back and now she stands in the gap for others as a prayer warrior.

Whenever you experience feelings of inadequacy, remember Barbara. She felt unqualified to be used by God even though, in His eyes, her identity was not tied to her actions and past mistakes. It took an encounter with God personally to realise that He had never left her. The only thing that God requires from us is our availability and willingness to be obedient. You will never know all the answers, have the best articulation with words, or make the right decisions, and you will make mistakes along the way. The Holy Spirit is our helper and guides us into all truth. It is written in Psalms 147:3 that

He heals the broken hearted, and binds up their wounds [healing their pain and comforting their sorrow].

You are about to reintroduce who you are to everyone who judged you, mocked you, and said you would amount to nothing. The rejection pushed you towards wanting to see your value and know your worth; it worked in your favour. I dare you to declare, "I am bold and fearless. My destiny helpers will find me and I am one step closer to my destiny." Now believe that destiny helpers have been assigned to help you with your God- given assignment and to turn your setbacks into comebacks.

I wrote a letter to my younger self, and it reads like this:

Dear younger self,

You were born to be a trail blazer. You are not the accumulation of your wrong choices in life. What you say to your reflection in the mirror will shape your future. Your beauty is not defined by the texture of your hair, the shape of your nose, or the size of your lips. Your imperfections make you beautiful. Your brokenness will give you a heart of compassion towards others so you can understand their pain. I know you are frustrated and looking for answers. Trust in God and He will show you the way. When people hurt you, refuse to live in resentment and forgive them. Every trial you face is a teacher, so make sure you pass the test. The enemy will fight you in the area he fears you the most.

Lust is deceiving and camouflages the pain. Don't waste your time wondering if he is the one. Do not become anxious or worry about tomorrow; your future is as bright as the day. Some will judge you based on your age, so stay true to your convictions, and choose to obey. Don't rush into loving someone before loving yourself first. Stop asking permission to be your authentic self, fearing to be judged by others. Not everyone will understand your journey, and that's ok. Do it anyway!

You are loved by an unfathomable God who has chosen you as His vessel. You have a gift that the world is waiting for. Be slow to speak, quick to listen, and slow to respond. The hidden treasure inside of you will be the key to unlocking destiny in others. Treasure every moment because they will eventually fade away. At an appointed time you will co-author with God and write your story. Dreams do come true, and you will plant the seed. Your voice will be used to sound the alarm in nations, as they give birth to their purpose in creation.

God is preparing you for the promise. You are becoming her... Your future self

PART 3

THE GREAT SPIRITUAL AWAKENING

Chapter Nine

DARE TO DREAM

A dream written down with a date becomes a goal. A goal broken down into steps becomes a plan. A plan backed by action makes your dreams come true. (Greg S. Reid)

In 2003, during my second year in my tourism development class, God gave me the words "hidden gems" and I stored them in my heart. At the time of hearing those words, I knew about God but I didn't have an intimate relationship with Him. I had no idea what to do with the vision God gave me, so I brushed off the idea. Fast forward fifteen years later, I began writing it down again and speaking to God about it. In Habakkuk 2:2-3 the Lord says *to write the vision and engrave it plainly on tablets so that the one who reads it will run. For the vision is yet for the appointed (future) time. It hurries towards the goal (of fulfilment), it will not fail. Even though it delays, wait (patiently) for it, because it will certainly come; it will not delay.*

Travel Gem was birthed in 2017. It is an inbound eco travel company in Cape Town that designs tailor-made packages to both local and international guests. Tsitsikamma is our favourite hidden gem. Sound familiar? That was where David's and my love story began. It's an adventure enthusiast's dream destination, where honeymooners escape to a secluded forest cabin, a nature's paradise surrounded by majestic forests. The words I heard all those years back was starting to take form and my dream was manifesting. The purpose of Travel Gem is to champion authenticity, encourage personal fulfilment, and leave a legacy behind of having educated the youth on leadership and the benefits of travel. Our vision is to be the leading authentic travel brand that offers meaningful tailor-made experiences, and a travel brand with a global footprint.

You are what you are exposed to. God promotes you and makes your dreams possible in order to pay it forward to the next generation that has given up on theirs. When your dream exists to better the life of others, you are building a legacy. When you plant a seed into someone else, you are guaranteed to get a reward for your obedience. We need to be the change we want to see. I am not perfect and God is still working on me; however, I have found that God used my insecurities and addictions to work in my favour, and this process has taught me that when you go through the fire, you will come out on the other side without a hint of smoke.

I have learnt to believe that if you can see it, then you can become it. Faith prompts us to step out and not allow our thinking to limit us. When we make the vision plain and write it down, we act in faith and remind God of His promises concerning our lives. I grew up believing that dreams were not meant to come true, and that they were merely an exercise to use your imagination while hoping for the best. What is the point in dreaming and not having the confidence that it can be realised? But, what if it is realised?

Growing up in a marginalised community where gangsterism was rife and dreams were just a fairy-tale, I had to dare to believe. About thirty years ago, I was the little girl sitting on the side of the road, looking up to the sky, and dreaming that one day I would be on an aircraft travelling the world. I have now had the privilege of flying people to the rest of the world and of bringing the world to Africa. I have lived the childhood dream that looked impossible once upon a time.

I still distinctly remember my first interview, at the age of twenty two, with South Africa's national airline carrier in 2006; it was an emotional day and left a footprint in my heart. I stood on my toes, challenged with remarks that I was too short, and fearing that I would not make the 1.58m criteria in height. However, if you are born to enter a door of opportunity, nothing can close that door. I was determined, and I was driven by a will to succeed at being an ambassador for my community and for future generations that would one day follow in my footsteps.

A new world was opened to me as I travelled to different countries and connected with the most amazing colleagues, passengers, cultures, and places, that impacted my life and changed my skewed perceptions. Everyone knows about the glamour of flying, but few know about the unspoken sacrifices attached to it. It became a lifestyle of layovers for three to six nights, having minimum time with your family, adapting to time zones, and persistent fatigue.

I was promoted to a senior crew member position ten years into my flying career, which pushed me to serve with excellence and to equip future leaders. This was all part of God's masterplan for me to acquire the necessary skills, knowledge, and understanding for what He was calling me to.

Then Coronavirus hit!

The coronavirus pandemic in 2020 caused the cancellation of all domestic, regional, and international flights, as the president closed all ports of entry by sea, road, and air to flatten the escalating upward curve of cases. Everything came to a standstill, and most parts of the world were put into lockdown. Our president Cyril Ramaphosa and his team had huge decisions to make in order to curb the spread of the virus, and they decided to instruct everyone to be in isolation at home. Only essential services were rendered. As the death toll rose globally, the virus spread to various hotspots, the schools were closed indefinitely, and parents stayed home to work from home. Small business owners and the travel industry were the most affected by the crisis we were facing.

I was directly affected by all the mayhem as travel bans brought the tourism industry to a standstill. I decided to invest most of my energy in learning new skills, writing as an aspiring author, and adapting to change. At the end of March, I received a message from the airline management that they were looking for voluntary crew to operate repatriation flights to Frankfurt, and to fly German nationals back to their respective countries. I purposed in my heart to be one of the crew members to serve our country, and after discussing it with my husband, we came into agreement on it. The repatriation flight to Frankfurt was departing from Cape Town and was bound to return to Johannesburg via Cairo, Egypt.

We went for pre-screening tests the week after receiving the initial message, followed by safety training and procedures, in preparation for the safe operation of the flight. I was scheduled to fly out at the end of that month. I had mixed feelings on the decision I made amidst the crisis we were facing as a country, yet somehow I just knew that I had to represent the country as an ambassador of South Africa and as a Kingdom representative. The call came on the scheduled day of departure: we were given our sign-on time, and reported for duty that evening. We covered the safety procedures and a briefing on the quarantine protocol. We cleared all the check points, the crew completed the necessary documentation at the airport, and we made our way to the aircraft. Before the passengers boarded, we donned our protective suits, face masks, and gloves, and assumed our working positions with pride as we welcomed our guests. Unlike a normal flight, we had to take extra safety precautions to ensure the passengers and crew were protected: we sanitised everything we could get our hands on. We arrived safely in Frankfurt after an 11-hour flight, and we stayed over for one night at a hotel in Mainz. On our return we had a stopover in Cairo to repatriate fellow South Africans. After the 7-hour flight back to Johannesburg, we spent thirteen days in quarantine at a hotel in close proximity to OR Tambo International Airport, before reuniting with our families.

God gave me a desire to dream bigger during my time in isolation. There was an increased intimacy that developed as I worshipped God every day, remaining in His presence, and yielding to His voice. I experienced a transition in my life, as God birthed new ideas, strategies, and revelation within me. I was unlocked during lockdown! I had to become still and pursue Him so that I could align myself to His timing. He got my attention alright!

As I sat in my room at our designated quarantine location, I reflected on the highlights of the flight: flying over Venice, the Greek islands, the Alps, and the most incredible sight of the Pyramids of Giza. I had a moment with God as He reminded me of the biblical event where Moses led the Israelites out of Egypt towards the Promised Land. He spoke to me that day as we flew over Egypt and I am convinced that something was ignited in me. This is a memory I will treasure forever. Sometimes we have to be still and 'see' what God is busy with so we don't miss it. Being able to see the pyramid with my own eyes gave me a insight concerning the events in the Bible. God sometimes has to intervene in our thinking and take us back to where it all started, so that He can give us renewed strength for what lies ahead.

When you dare to dream, the opportunities are endless. The lockdown unlocked kingdom potential in those who were sensitive to His voice during the pandemic. I was reminded that, even though we were in the wilderness, God was still speaking and doing His good works, behind the scenes. His promises have not changed, although it can become easy, in such circumstances, to lose focus and start murmuring along the way. This can become a stumbling block for the move of God.

There were so many uncertainties during this time as businesses were collapsing and my flying career was on the verge of coming to an end, post- lockdown. However, I did not stop dreaming, because I was expectant for a total reset to take place. My career may be my resource, but God is my Source. The end of the road can very well be the beginning of something new. When you allow God to be the author of your life, His script becomes a most beautiful story, which He writes piece by piece. A dream cannot be birthed if there is no seed of belief to create the right environment for it to grow. You need to dream and believe God for bigger things, if you want Him to increase your capacity, and if you want to discover your gifts from above. It is your God-given gifts that sustain you to give birth to your visions, not your career or your education.

Being Sensitive to the Holy Spirit

In the beginning of January 2018, God gave me the desire to write a book. It seemed far-fetched and impossible at the time because, while growing up, I was not exposed to authors and entrepreneurs in my circle of friends. It was just a childhood dream.

Celebrities write books. Creative people write books. At least, that's what I believed to be true. I have a collection of motivational books in my personal library written by international authors, yet success stories from people in impoverished communities are lacking. Our stories matter and need a platform to be heard.

I stumbled upon an advertisement on Facebook for a master class in Johannesburg, hosted by Darren August, for aspiring authors. I knew I had to attend. I secured my spot for the class online and booked my ticket to Johannesburg for attendance on 3 February, a day before my birthday. I flew to Johannesburg the day before the event, and stayed over at my friend Daphne's place in Pretoria. She dropped me at the venue on the Saturday and my journey of writing began. I quickly realised that I was on an assignment when the Lord gave me a word of knowledge for one of the women who attended. When I walked past her in the ladies' bathroom, I knew that God had set her apart so that she could receive the word. He will do whatever it takes to get his people's attention. She confirmed that the word was indeed true. God was awakening her to purpose.

I exited the bathroom and sat down in the front row of the class. I wore a bright shot red jacket and I was the only attendee from Cape Town with hand luggage. I stood out like a sore thumb. Amanda, the woman whom God had laid on my heart, sat next to me, and the exhilarating master class for aspiring authors commenced. My dream was ignited and came to life that day. The gift inside of me was unlocked.

Amanda gave me a lift to the airport, and I gave her a brand new book that I had in my handbag. It turned out to be exactly what she needed in the season she found herself. We sat in the car worshipping God, tears streaming down our faces, and soaking in every moment of our divine connection. The joy of the Lord flooded my heart. I then made my way to the check-in counters, was issued with my boarding pass, and boarded my flight back home to Cape Town. My obedience in going to the master class in another city pushed me towards my destiny. We have been innately designed to soar.

That sequence of events was divinely orchestrated to birth this book, in order to release a sound to a generation who has been desensitised by sexual sin, and to pull them out of pornography addiction and push them towards discovering their God-given purpose. Amanda is also an author, and she has since published her poetry book and is impacting lives, one generation at a time.

If your dream does not scare you, it's not big enough! When you find your purpose, you find your gift. What you say to yourself is the difference between being successful and remaining stagnant. What you endure is as significant as the promise or end goal, because it serves a purpose. When you procrastinate, you are not stewarding your time well. I am sure that you have had a desire to start something new, but you failed because of fear and not knowing where to start. You will never be ready to step out! You should just do it and believe that you have what it takes to accomplish what you set out to do.

What you sow, you reap, and you cannot expect a harvest if you do not put in the work. It starts with a seed planted in the ground of an abundant supply of trust and faith. Discover what you are good at, and write it down. Listen to the compliments of your most trusted friends; this gives you a good indication of your strengths and talents.

Make your vision simple, set realistic goals and timelines, put time aside, and take action. It may be to complete your studies, overcome your fear of driving, write a blog, or even start a women's ministry. The only person stopping you, is you. Dare to dream!

Chapter Ten

ANSWERING THE CALL

For many are called (invited, summoned), but few are chosen. (Matthew 22:14, AMP)

What are you most frustrated about? What angers you? What do you find yourself often complaining about?

These are hints to what you are called to. Is it giving to the poor with a compassionate heart, teaching the youth, giving hope and encouragement to the broken hearted with your smile, or empowering others for their destiny? Every time God calls you it's away from comfort. He calls you from comfort to chaos to see if you will trust Him to be peaceful in the middle of the storm. If you find yourself in a struggle, it is your training ground, and He allows it because He has faith in you that you will pass the test. The highest calling on your life isn't necessarily being a pastor or missionary, it's glorifying God and serving others in whatever work God has called you to do.

Do not despise where you are; it forms part of your journey. My job as a senior flight attendant was my training ground for my assignment and calling. Whenever I conducted a safety briefing with my crew, God was preparing me to minister to the hearts of people. When I made announcements on the Public Address (PA) system, I gained the confidence to speak to global leaders, CEO's, presidents, ministers, celebrities, and kingdom influencers. I now look back and see the pieces of the puzzle fitting together. If you have to serve in a job to gain the necessary skill and expertise for your kingdom assignment, then do it to the best of your ability, and pray for spiritual mentors to pour into your life so you can move into your calling, and also assist the next generation that is waiting on God's timing for their own destiny to unfold.

At some point in my own life I felt as if I was in the fight of my life; my flight schedule would only allow me to attend Sunday services when I had a day off, and I was criticised by some believers for not being able to attend all the church events. I told my husband that I was going to record my responses so that I didn't have to repeat myself every Sunday. I just wanted to worship and be in God's presence, and not be inundated with questions. There is an expectancy at some corporate gatherings that if you don't fit in with the church culture, then you are doing something wrong. Have you ever tried fitting a piece of a puzzle into a section where it doesn't belong? No matter how hard you try to manoeuvre it in, it can't help but stand out. Being overlooked and not fitting in may be a blessing and not a curse. God chooses and uses the least likely vessels to represent Him on this earth.

I was a full time student, full time wife, and full time servant of God. I was planning women's events, hosting prayer meetings at our place, and arranging outreaches in the community, in between my flight schedules. The believers who criticized me the most were the ones who were neither serving in ministry nor fulfilling their purpose. In spite of this, I enjoyed every moment of my assignment at that time and I believe that God's grace was empowering me for that season. Before entering a time of rest, I learned valuable lessons. I paused. I reflected. I transitioned.

God gave me a vision two years ago that He would shift me into the next season, and it has come into fulfilment as I write this. The disruption from the crisis presented the opportunity and platform to seek Him more. God is surely up to something when He leaves the ninety nine to go for the one.

If you are seeking God for direction and have come to a crossroads, hold on. Help is on the way. God is anointing and appointing people into their positions, and a new remnant of born again believers are rising up.

When you answer the call, there is bound to be resistance as you carry a message that the world needs to hear and that God has given uniquely to you. This should not deter you from reaching your full capacity. You will be robbing generations of your gift if you allow fear to dictate your decisions. You need to be bold and courageous when you step into whom God created you to be. The voices of the enemy may attempt to draw you away through intimidation, and you will need to be focused. God equips those whom He calls to do His work through the 3 P's: Preparation (trials we face), Positioning (process we endure) for our Purpose (aligned with God's purpose). In the book of Esther, God says *And who knows whether you have attained royalty for a time such as this (and for this very purpose).* (Esther 4:14, AMP)

It is God's intention for you to discover your gifts and talents and then make use of them. Every human being was born with gifts that need to be stirred and become active before they can serve their purpose. Everything you were born to become is already inside of you; it is not something that still needs to be attained. Nobody can give it to you, nor can it be purchased, but in order for the gifts to be stirred up, you need to seek God. Some may be called to function in ministries such as: giving through outreaches, preaching the word, prophesying, teaching, evangelising, or healing, but your gifts are not only required in a church setting. More importantly, they are required in the marketplace, where they are needed the most. God can use you as His vessel in the workplace, your business, your family, at the local coffee shop, or in a circle of friends. You may have the correct gift, but be using it in the wrong environment. The effectiveness of the church is not just in the gifts that are in operation, but in their functional environment. It would be a tragedy if you had the right weapons but you were in the wrong war.

What many religious folk deem to be 'normal' is based on attending church on a Sunday morning, and does not include going out of the four corners of the building to make disciples. This is not necessarily the full description of your assignment or a true reflection of the Kingdom of God. God chooses you based on where He needs you the most, which is not limited to serving in one capacity. If you are a brilliant speaker and know how to get a crowd, it is a gift that God has given you to be exercised on a particular platform to infiltrate secular systems with a Kingdom agenda. *For the kingdom of God is not a matter of eating and drinking [what one likes], but of righteousness and peace and joy in the Holy Spirit.* (Romans 14:17, AMP)

When you empower and equip others, you are influencing God's Kingdom. We are citizens of His Kingdom and, as His ambassadors, we take His Kingdom with us wherever we go, we reflect His nature, and we make disciples. The Kingdom is more about being than doing. The great commission the Body of Christ has been given is to go and teach all nations, and to baptise them in the name of the Father, the Son and the Holy Spirit.

The church is only one function of the Kingdom of God; it is where you are equipped with kingdom principles to go, as kingdom influencers, into all sectors of society, to impact industries as young professionals, and to change world systems and businesses. 'Seeking the Kingdom' (Matthew 6:33) means finding out how God wants things done, how He wants us to treat people, how He wants us to act in situations, what He wants us to do with our finances, what kind of attitude we should have, and how to flow in our God-given purpose. This process is governed by having a nature that is pleasing to God with its accompanying God-pleasing attitude that you adopt after you have left the church building. Service and discipleship require you to serve where you are, whether it's your local store or at the nursery. Serving is a privilege, not an obligation. Serving is selfless and not to be carried out with an expectation of being seen or applauded publicly. Whenever you serve, strive for excellence. The following story testifies of the application of this principle and the goodness of God.

A few years back I travelled to Dakar, Senegal, for work and met one of the locals by the name of Ngala who sold arts and crafts at a local craft market. I was having lunch with colleagues when I asked one of them to accompany me to the craft market. I felt led by the Holy Spirit to go to a particular craft store, where poverty was the reality, and this is where I met Ngala. He spoke only broken English, but we managed to get our message across. In the middle of the conversation, I asked him if I could pray for him, and he agreed. The presence of God was tangible as he allowed us to speak into his life, and with tears in his eyes, he experienced the love of God. I spoke to him about how much Jesus loved him and wanted to be in relationship with him.

I kept all the pictures and memories of that trip. On three occasions over the following three years I went back to visit, to see his progress, and find out what God was doing in his life. The seed had been planted, and the author and finisher of our faith allowed it to sprout and grow. I saved his number so that we could stay in contact and I could help him to keep the faith. We exchanged pictures of our families, and he shared when his wife was expecting a baby. God can use you to reach someone on a different continent for His will to be done. He is seeking your willingness to be used by Him, and He will do the rest. The above account is merely one instance of my own experience. God calls each individual differently to glorify Him.

Another account of a personal kingdom assignment was during my layover in Australia. Perth was my least favourite destination to fly to because of the time change. I was awake when I was supposed to be sleeping and vice versa. I would have preferred to swop my flight and go to New York, and I attempted exactly to do that. I tried to swop with many of my colleagues but had no success.

The day of my flight to Perth arrived. We completed our safety briefings, and cleared security to prepare the aircraft for our passengers. I knew that there was a greater purpose for me to be on that flight. During our stay at the hotel, I received a message from one of my colleagues that she was having suicidal thoughts. I had spoken to her on the flight prior to the check-in, and I encouraged her after she reached out to me. She was stuck in sexual sin. I could relate to her pain because I had been there. She wanted to jump off the balcony that evening. She was held hostage in her room by the harmful thoughts that flooded her mind. I forwarded messages to prayer warriors to stand in agreement with me, and God came through for her. I led her to Christ that very evening, and blessed her with a brand new Bible that I had packed before my trip. When God calls us to go and make disciples, it's not about our comfort, or our preferences. It's about His perfect will.

You experience God in different seasons of your life, and sometimes have to eradicate any default thinking that puts Him in a box. The kingdom lifestyle is about reflecting His character in a dying world through a life of obedience. If we are to be true bondservants of Christ, we are ambassadors of God in every area of our lives: *And God blessed them, and God said unto them, be fruitful, and multiply, and replenish the earth, and subdue it: and have dominion over the fish of the seas, and over the fowl of the air, and over every thing that moveth upon the earth.* (Genesis 1:28, KJV) The kingdom lifestyle becomes part of who we are; it is not merely an act, a religious ritual, or a man-made tradition, but an expression of our whole being and life as worship, being in His will, and living a life of surrender.

The coronavirus outbreak in the year 2020 has caused a spiritual awakening. Facing a pandemic as a country and the isolation during lockdown has prompted us to do some introspection as we escaped our busy lives and learned again to appreciate our time with loved ones. It taught us to be intentional about where we invest our time. Rest is one of the most spiritual things you can do as a believer. Let that sink in! You need to set time aside to stop and reflect in order to get a new perspective on the season you find yourself in, and assess your current assignment/s. I experienced some of my most intimate moments with God in the 'secret place', behind the shut door of my prayer room, during this time. It takes a "yes" from within. Love always wins and draws us near to our Abba Father. To seek His face and proclaim His goodness, you often have to say "no" to others so you can say "yes" to Him.

We should not wait for the addiction to be broken, or the proof of liberty, before we act in faith and believe His promises. It is our duty to trust

God and follow His guidelines to set us free. God calls us in the midst of our struggles and addictions and does not wait until we are perfect before releasing us to do what He has called us to. He is the one who does a perfect work within us and works it out for our good. Those around us may look at our behaviour (outwardly) and sin, but God looks at our hearts (inwardly) and sees destiny.

Whenever you enter a new season, you have to let go of the old. It is impractical to do a new thing in your life while you are holding on to past hurt and disappointment. God wants to unlock kingdom potential within you. He is all-knowing, and He knows your struggles and addictions that influence your free will to choose. He gives you the ability to make decisions to choose life or death. The good news is that you were designed to be an overcomer and to live a victorious life.

One of my biggest fears became a reality when my father was diagnosed with stage four stomach cancer in April 2019 after he had retired the previous year. I remember receiving the news when my husband phoned me during my layover in Accra, Ghana, on my 7-day flight en route to Washington DC. My husband's words were, "I wanted to wait until you back home, but I have to let you know that dad was diagnosed with cancer." I sat on the bed for a couple of minutes, staring into blank space and struggling to digest every word I had just heard ... and hoping that it was a bad dream that would soon end. It felt like someone had just ripped out my heart, and put it back again. I wrestled with God in my quiet time as I tried to make peace with the diagnosis. I had prayed for my father's salvation for years and had waited on God's appointed time. Finally, when I answered God's call and walked in obedience, a month before my father's passing, we led him to Christ and baptised him at our family home. Obedience is better than sacrifice. I witnessed his spiritual transformation despite his frail body and a swollen leg caused by a Deep Vein Trombosis (DVT) and a clot that had spread. He was at peace, knowing that eternal life awaited him. When we pray for our families, our prayers often are not answered the way we hope. God orchestrates answers through His infinite wisdom.

During my father's illness, I went for a check-up at my local gynaecologist. She discovered two huge fibroids, and I was advised to go for a myomectomy, a major surgical procedure that entails making an incision through the skin on the lower abdomen, to remove the fibroids. We scheduled a time for the operation, and a few weeks later I was admitted into hospital where it was removed. My C-section scar is my reminder that God's ways are higher than our ways.

The day after I was discharged, my father passed away and went to be with the Lord in eternal peace. He had gained a heart of repentance, and followed the example Jesus Christ set before Him. He was not healed of the cancer, and it is not my place to question God, but to trust His perfect will. We might not understand the reason we go through these trials, but I believe there is a purpose, and ultimately, God uses everything to further His plan.

There are often details and significance in our journeys that makes no sense at the time. For instance, some people who did not understand my journey bombarded me with questions after one year of marriage by asking, "Are you planning to have a baby?" or "Don't worry, it will happen in God's time." I would have my responses ready just in case I needed them. One day I made up my mind and decided I owed nobody an explanation. It was part of my testimony. Whether it was infertility, barrenness, the ovulation process, or God saying "Not now", I was at peace. If it should happen tomorrow or three weeks from now, so shall it be. Stereotypes should be placed back in the box where they belong with the rest of the 'labels'. They have reached their expiry date. We don't have control of what's asked of us, but we have the ability to react or not.

The enemy will try to use our circumstances to pull us away from our call, but the purposes of God will not take us where He cannot sustain us. After my father's passing, I was more intentional than ever about fulfilling my purpose. My father couldn't accomplish half of the things that were predestined for him because he was not awakened or exposed to greater things. He had succumbed to the environment he was in, and was surrounded by destiny killers. He abandoned his dreams because of his decisions, and merely fought for survival, emotionally, physically, spiritually, and mentally. The death of a loved one has a unique way of bringing things into perspective, whether it's someone that you know, or someone dear to a friend that you are supporting. It's as if your whole life flashes in front of you. At least, that is how it was for me.

God clothes us with supernatural strength when we give our grief to Him. He is our comforter, and He mourns with us during the process. He alone can mend our broken hearts. I choose not to mourn on birthdays, or milestone dates, or on significant days that have meaning, but to celebrate my father's life every opportunity I get. I remember how proud he was at my ordination, and I will cling to the memories. I was so proud of my father and the decision he made to be rebirthed in Christ after wrestling for many years. His name, Peter, means 'rock' and his fighting spirit bore testimony to it. He left his mark in the hearts of everyone who knew him. He was loved and respected by many in the community, and I will continue with the legacy he left behind, which is to be a voice for the marginalised, and to work hard for what you want to accomplish.

The assignments God gives us are not dependant on favourable circumstances. They are strictly dependant on obedience. The same day I received the news of my father's diagnosis, I was assigned by the Holy Spirit to go to the office of the Ghanaian Minister of States, and to pray for her. God specifically laid her on my heart. We had previously chatted over the phone when she was in charge of the tourism office during my previous travels to Ghana, and she had since been promoted. Before receiving the instruction from God, my colleague Qumi and I explored the local markets in Accra. Qumi was a prayer warrior herself and ended up joining me on my kingdom expedition. She didn't ask any questions. We were in unity and armed with a prayer strategy.

We arranged for a local taxi, followed the directions given, got lost, and found our way again. When you have a divine assignment there are always obstacles. When we walked into the entrance of Cathy's office, her secretary advised us that she was expecting me. I released the word God gave me, and God used me that day to confirm what He had already spoken to Cathy. If I had walked in the flesh and allowed my emotions to consume me, I would have grieved the Holy Spirit. He would have chosen someone else to be His vessel. There were many incidents after that, where God supernaturally intervened during my travels.

Whether you are a thirty five year old man with three children, a pastor's wife not knowing her purpose, or a forty eight year old woman living in regret, regardless of your circumstances, God will ask what you did with the talents He gave you. Did you use them or did you bury them? You have the free will to make the right decision that will set up the next generation for victory.

I am expectant for the future and the unveiling of your purpose and destiny. Believe with me. Expectation births opportunity. I pray that the blurred signs at the crossroads will finally start to make sense and that they will assist you to discern the direction you should take. As you partner with

God, you will eventually shift from being a victim of your circumstance to being a co-labourer with Christ.

Chapter Eleven

RAISING CHILDREN OF DESTINY

Train up a child in the way he should go [teaching him to seek God's wisdom and will for his abilities and talents], and when he is old he will not depart from it. (Proverbs 22:6, AMP)

Jesus was birthed according to prophecy after the angel Gabriel appeared to a virgin girl named Mary who lived in Nazareth. The angel of the Lord revealed that she would conceive a son after the Holy Spirit fell upon her and the power of God overshadowed her in a cloud of glory, and that she would name him Jesus. Mary received the word by faith and the angel left her. She was chosen as a vessel to raise the promised child of destiny who would be the Saviour of the world. The responsibility that rested upon her was not a light one, yet she chose to obey. Called to preserve the seed of the promise, and rear Him for his destiny, she named her child for His purpose – that of Saviour.

The name you give your children carries power and great spiritual significance. For instance, the name *Nabal* in Hebrew means 'fool', and this was the legacy he left behind after threatening David over an insult, and he was ultimately killed by God.

You should not have the mentality that you are raising your children for yourself. You are rather to raise them for the purposes of God. You are to steer them into their purpose by reflecting God's love, praying for their friends, and praying for Godly influences in their life. Start to pray for their sexual purity when they are still young.

Parenthood is not only a privilege, it is a spiritual obligation to raise your seed based on biblical foundations. Have you ever asked a child, "What do you want to be when you grow up?", and received the response, "I want to be a doctor", "I want to be a lawyer "or "I want to be a pilot". Is that it? Surely someone must have passed down that exclusive list from previous generations. Do not feel defeated if they do not make the cut and rather desire to be a ground-breaking scientist, social entrepreneur, or anointed preacher. Their God-given purpose is so much greater!

As you co-parent with God, He gives you guidance on how to raise your child. You have to die to your own will, and accept His will for your children. When you don't have a vision for your own life, the chances are that your children will have blurred vision too, but they can be trained to stir up their gifts from a young age. Teach them to speak the truth at all costs. Teach them right from wrong, and walk in righteousness yourself as an example. Your obedience will lead to their obedience, despite the circumstances they were born into. Ideally, the father is the head of the household and submits to God first, before he lays down the Godly principles to be followed. In the absence of the father, God remains the final authority to consult for guidance.

He will place support structures or destiny helpers in your life.

There are moments when hurtful words are spoken in anger and frustration. Always walk in forgiveness when this occurs so that the enemy does not get a foothold in your lives. Disciplining requires you to correct in love. Fear of failure and disappointment should not deter you from pursuing God-inspired relationships with your children. Pray for wisdom, knowledge, and understanding at all times.

Four years ago, I received a prophecy from the Jamaican author, Dr. Patricia Morgan. She is a professional consultant in education, the author of *Battle of the Seed*, and a mother with a prophetic heart. It reads as follows: *May you be fruitful in the Lord, and may God use you to anoint the Body of Christ, and to bless the people of God! Wisdom I pray for you as you Raise Children of Destiny!* I have stored this prophetic word in my heart. It is coming into fulfilment as I co-labour with God to equip the future generation. The battle for the seed is real: parents are fighting an anti-Christ adversary for the future of the next generation. The secular education system is threatening to take Godly principles away, therefore it is imperative that we teach our children God's unwavering truth. Teach them the reverential fear of the Lord, to discern God's purpose for their life, and to speak it into existence. If you leave it to chance, they may never experience who they were created to be. Start with a commitment to pray for your seed and for the promises of God to be fulfilled in their lives. Do not push your personal agendas and desires onto them, especially if they are not in alignment with the purposes of God. Raise them up to be future leaders. Do not compare siblings with one another; God has given each one unique attributes and personalities. Compliment them, don't criticise them, and do not break their spirit. Build up their confidence. A spoken word can plant a seed of hope and endurance, and can unlock hidden potential.

Meet Clarissa

She is a single, divorced mother raising two boys aged eleven and six. Clarissa did not leave her previous marriage on good terms and is bound by her past hurts. Simon, her eleven-year-old son, is deeply affected by the departure of his father and is acting up by smoking marijuana. Simon feels alone, rejected, and unloved, and has no sense of purpose. His mother focused on her own pain and the lack of interest from her ex-husband, and made decisions based on aspects of her dysfunctional relationships. She became tired of fighting the same battles and struggling to get to the root problem. Clarissa has met someone else in the interim and has introduced him to the boys, but Clarissa needed a Godly intervention to prevent the enemy from using her situation to abort her children's destiny.

Her surrender to God's will came at a cost as she had to 'die to self', find healing for her wounded soul, and confess the word of God over her family. She is now committed to the covenant promises of God regardless of how she feels.

We should continue to pray for Godly men and mentors to step up and impart vision to the children of destiny. We need to adapt our thinking and rein in the power of misdirected generational thinking. If you are a first generation believer, it begins with you to change the trajectory of broken cycles and poverty mindsets. It takes one person in the family to receive God's redemptive love and break the curses of past generations.

Leaders from older generations should impart their wisdom into the younger so that they can take over the baton and operate in their gifts as God intended them to. 1 Timothy 4:12 says *Let no man despise thy youth, but be thou an example.* A spiritual mentor can be described as a wise, trusted counsellor or teacher. Jesus mentored His disciples during His ministry on earth.

Ps Chana, my spiritual mentor who has passed the age of 60, dedicates her time and resources towards imparting wisdom to younger leaders who have been given a heavenly mandate in this new era. There is no need for the older generation to feel intimidated by young ministry leaders. The focus should be on the generational legacy: empowering God's future vessels to take the Kingdom by force, imparting wisdom, and anointing the leaders to their assigned ministries. Impactful leaders identify other potential leaders and equip them to excel in their spheres of influence. It is every generation's responsibility to develop the next generation to leave a leadership legacy behind.

The above Kingdom principles are not only limited to your own seed but also to the spiritual mentees God has assigned to you. As a vessel of God raising children of destiny, you are required to pour into intercessors, young professionals, aspiring preachers, and those who have been set apart to be ordained by God. The only way to break down altars erected by a perverse generation is to reintroduce holiness and purity. Make worship a lifestyle and not a ritual of singing hymns at corporate gatherings. Invest time for devotion and praying as a family to withstand the fiery darts of the enemy.

We have been bestowed with a mandate of stewardship to glorify God through the way we raise our children, who are, in effect, His children. A new era has come to restore families back to God's original intention, to replace fear with perfect love, to change curses to blessings, and to exchange broken covenants for a covenant with God. The enemy wants us to be oblivious to what is happening behind the scenes. The lies. The deception. Human trafficking and abortion. All are plots from the enemy to wipe out the future generations so that the promises of God are not fulfilled. He has devised his master plan to kill and has been strategic about it. God knows the plan for your child's life, and the *accuser of the brethren* (satan) also does. We are the gatekeepers for the children of destiny. God has a divine purpose for every child under the sun, and has given each one a desire to answer their unique call at an appointed time. There is a battle for the seed. He has chosen you to be a destiny carrier!

Chapter Twelve

CONNECTING THE DOTS TO PURPOSE

Being confident of this very thing, that he which hath begun a good work in you will perform it until the day of Jesus Christ. (Philippians 1:6, KJV)

Purpose is the reason something or someone was created. We can only be fruitful with what God entrusts to us when we discover our purpose and know who we are called to be. Many are still seeking purpose and looking for it in the wrong place. It is not something tangible that someone can claim to give you. The primary reason we miss it is because we were led to believe man-made teachings that pushed us away from purpose instead of pulling us towards it. Everything that we have endured thus far was for a purpose. I discovered mine when I helped others unveil theirs. Purpose is determined by God and destiny is determined by the choices we make. God created the birds, the sea, animal life, and everything that has breath, with purpose in mind. The purpose of a chair is for people to sit on it and not for a means of self-defence. Well, one can use it for that purpose, but it won't be ideal. When we do not know why we were designed a particular way, we waste years of our lives failing to fulfil the assignment we were created for. Wouldn't it be terrifying to know that we have never performed at the level of God's intention for us – an intention He conceived even before we were intricately formed in our mothers' womb? If we fail to walk in our destiny, we are contributing to the decay of a generation who are waiting for us to manifest ourselves to the world.

God is not surprised by the family you were born into, the community you live in, or the limitations you were exposed to as children. They were all meticulously pre-planned to strengthen your character, and to give you a testimony to share for a greater purpose.

The pursuit of purpose attracts great warfare. You may ask why did God allow what happened to me? We may never have the answer, but we must trust His sovereignty and not allow our thoughts to be elevated over His perfect thoughts. What we do know is that He will never leave us nor forsake us, and that He will be with us through every storm, even in the midst of His silence. A wilderness season of abandonment was never intended to kill us but to strengthen us. I had many failed attempts on my journey with God when He called me to minister to women. It is important to separate an event of failure from who you are as an individual. Failure will prepare you; there is always a lesson in it so that you never lose. You were created for something bigger than yourself, and the trials are moulding you for the next season. If you want to succeed in any area of your life, you need to submit it to God. He won't fix something He never gave you permission to start.

Destiny Helpers and Destiny Killers

Destiny is the divine blueprint of our lives and there are two kinds of people we will encounter in our lifetime: destiny helpers and destiny killers. God places destiny helpers in our lives to help us achieve our dreams. Jesus needed John the Baptist, Mordecai was the destiny helper of Esther, and Aaron was a destiny helper to Moses when he led the Israelites out of Egypt.

Destiny Helpers - Mary and Elizabeth

Mary was Elizabeth's destiny helper. The angel of the Lord appeared to Mary and told her that her cousin Elizabeth, who was called barren, had conceived a son in her old age and was in her sixth month. Luke 1:37 proclaims, *For with God nothing is ever impossible and no word from God shall be without power or impossible of fulfilment.* Mary arose and went to the town in Judah where Zachariah and Elizabeth resided. When she entered their house and greeted them, fixing her attention on Elizabeth, the baby leaped in Elizabeth's womb by the power of the Holy Spirit, upon hearing Mary's voice.

Some scholars say that Elizabeth was in hiding because of her old age and that she feared the baby would be stillborn, until Mary knocked on the door. It was revealed to Elizabeth, through the leaping son in her womb, that Mary was going to give birth to Jesus. Jesus was later baptised by Elizabeth's child, John the Baptist, as events unfolded. The significance of these events changed history and we are bearing the fruit of it today. When Mary hastily chose to be obedient and embrace her purpose to be used by God, the miracles of the births of John and Jesus were the results, yet these were mere shadows of what was to come. God has chosen you to be someone's Mary or Elizabeth to help them to fulfil their destiny. You have a unique personality and passion, and unique attributes that compliment those of your destiny helper. Your spiritual DNA matches that of another woman, and it has carefully been designed for the leaping to occur and for your respective assignments to be birthed. Do not miss the opportunity to realign broken generational cycles and to be part of history in the making. When everyone says it is impossible, God demonstrates the possible.

Destiny Killers

Destiny killers are individuals who frustrate the call of God on our lives, and they may come disguised as friends who have our best interests at heart. They become envious when we succeed and venture into new things. A destiny killer tries to steal our ability to focus on the goal ahead. Some people are tempted to abort their dreams because they are surrounded by destiny killers who do not value them. We need to be discerning and watch out for destiny killers, as they may suck the life out of us. These individuals may have ill feelings towards us, or they may carry offenses, but we are to be cautious not to harbour unforgiveness. It is our duty to keep our hearts in check from any root of bitterness and strife if we want our prayers answered. When we stay focused, our emotions will eventually catch up with us. We need to make up our minds not to waste time in unhealthy relationships.

Battle Scars

Wounds and scars are there as a reminder. Our wounds serve a purpose. Someone is benefiting and getting help from our wounds. Jesus wants access to our pain and struggles. If we could fix ourselves, there would have been no need for Jesus to die. Physical wounds are easier to see when you have sustained an injury and are bleeding from a particular area. Internal wounds are hidden from the next person and cannot be detected by merely looking at someone. This is the reason many people are suffering from depression, and one may not notice if one is not focusing on the mental health and emotional triggers. Managing the mind (will and emotions), the soul, and the body, is essential to overall well-being.

Many have taught themselves to hide their emotional scars to avoid being vulnerable, when the freedom lies in doing the exact opposite. Our scars are a beautiful expression of what we conquered. It was the grace of God that kept us for a time such as this, to remind us where our help comes from. Our scars are never arbitrary, they are there to help unlock someone else's destiny with our transparency and testimony. God always gets the glory from saving us from ourselves.

If you have been gracefully broken, your value does not depreciate. If you tear up a cash note, step on it in the mud, and put it back together, the value does not change. In the same way, you may go through times of great difficulty, but when God takes you out of the dark pit, strips away your 'old self', and makes you whole, and you surrender all that you are to take on all that He is, you become a new creation of undiminished value. The battle scars of past hurts are treasures to be embraced. They form a part of you, so you might as well tell your story and be bold about it. The more you hide secret sins, the more they haunt you and control your future decisions. An absent or abusive father causes some of the worst trauma and deepest wounds, but trauma doesn't define you, only God does. The antidote to darkness is light, and when you begin to deal with your traumatic experiences, God can start the healing process. After healing, there may still be scars, but they are testimonies to your victory.

You will receive a double reward for every person who cheated on you, abused you, and betrayed you, when you change your focus to the purpose and not the perpetrator. Every tactic of the enemy meant to destroy you will return to sender, if only you put your trust in God. God's outcome will not be based on how you feel, but based on your act of obedience.

Education Is Not Enough To Discover Your Purpose

It gives me great joy when a person discovers and walks in his or her purpose amidst their circumstances. It is the reason I get up in the morningto help others find their 'why'. There is more to life than getting up in the morning, having breakfast (if any at all), going to work, getting the job done, receiving a salary that your employer thinks you are worth, driving home, preparing supper, having some family time if time allows, and getting to bed early, only to repeat it all again. If you have children, you drive them to school, pick them up again, make sure they are fed and their homework gets done, and tuck them into bed. Weekends are just too short. Before you know it, you have to prepare for Monday again.

If you are a student, you may spend five years studying for a degree. After graduating, you are not quite sure if it's the field you want to be in. The unemployment rate in the country is already staggering as it is. The probability of enrolling for a course at university that enhances your God- given gift is questionable. You need to do your research for the particular industry you wish to be in, or you may end up choosing the wrong subjects.

Ironically, I failed this research methodology. The following year, I dusted myself off and tried again. I learned a valuable lesson: even if your life takes a detour, you will eventually be right where you are supposed to be. Stay the course.

My graduation for my Master's degree was delayed by one year because one of the supervisors failed to hand it in before the deadline. When I was finally ready to submit, my appointed external assessor went on a sabbatical. We had issues with the editor, and it was just a mess. It took me five years to finish my full thesis, and what a rollercoaster of events it turned out to be! But God takes our mess and turns it into our message. Before you can move onto the next season of your life, there are pre-requisites you have to fulfil. If you have not yet arrived, trust the process. Stay the course. Giving up is not an option. I understand your pain. You will need more than your education to complete your assignment. The moment you discover your why, you can then start to unmask your purpose.

Road to Entrepreneurship

My desire for women to know their purpose unlocked the name 'Purpose Mid-wife', meaning 'A God-fearing woman who births purpose in others'. I help individuals unlock their kingdom potential so that they can discover their gifts and purpose without wasting years of their lives unfulfilled. I also give them tools to turn their passions into profit. You need to know that what you are about to embark on is bigger than yourself. For me, transitioning into becoming a purpose coach happened organically. I had a lingering passion for uncovering purpose and derived fulfilment from encouraging others. I invested in a few courses and started my journey as a coach during lockdown. It was my choice to learn to build up the next generation through equipping and empowering them to walk in their God- given purpose. You can only go as far as your mind is willing to take you.

Entrepreneurial skills were not passed down from my family line, hence I was a first generation kingdom entrepreneur. I had no reference or template from anyone who had led a successful business. It was foreign to me. I had to learn and research everything through reading books, and attending online classes, workshops, and network events for entrepreneurs. I was always drawn to starting my own business, and I just needed to step out in faith.

If you have a business idea, don't allow finances to deter you. The more you think about it, the more you sow seeds of doubt and open yourself to seeing a million reasons for it to fail. It's like learning to drive. At first, you get behind the steering wheel, and you pray you don't hit a pedestrian. I was extremely fearful when I drove for the first time. I hired a driving instructor so that I could become more confident on the road. My turns were wide around the bend, and I drove into the pavement a couple of times. More than ten years ago, I was parked in a parking area, and as I reversed, I scratched the side of a white car with my brand new Toyota Yaris that I had saved up for some time. I panicked. I drove off, and I could literally feel my heart pounding like a drum. What was I thinking? A guy who happened to be passing by witnessed the whole incident and took a photo of my number plate. When I got home I received the call that I dreaded. I apologised, and I contacted my insurance provider to cover the damages. This did not stop me from getting back into the car and being more cautious. There was no way I could bubble wrap the vehicle to protect it from damages.

The same applies to starting a business. You might fail a few times, but eventually you will become an expert in your field to help others. Business is a game, and you have to be an active participant. It's about being consistent when you don't see immediate results. It has its ups and downs, but most importantly, you have control over the success you want to achieve. If you follow the road signs and stick to the rules, you will remain on the right course. Get a coach to activate your gifts and bring out the best in you. You have something unique that can add value to someone's life.

I encourage every millennial to surround themselves with successful people, listen to their mistakes, and also pay attention to their road to success. Don't say a word. Just absorb and apply what is applicable to where you currently find yourself. Invest in your personal development by learning a new skill and networking with likeminded individuals.

Although it requires hard work to be successful, it gives you a sense of value and meaning. The small things count, such as planning your day ahead with the goals you want to achieve. No-one becomes an instant millionaire. As a flight attendant during some of my layovers on my ten day Washington flights, I would write down my vision and goals, and I would finish assignments towards my master's degree. Ok! Let me be honest. I would indulge in lazing at the pool on one of those days and on some trips, such as the one to Ghana, I would balance it out with sightseeing and exploring the local culture.

I was focused and intentional on pursuing purpose and doing whatever it took to invest in my business which, at time of writing, is three years old. I adopted an attitude of serving in ministry, running my travel business, and executing my job with excellence. I worked with the resources that I had, even though I couldn't be physically present at all times. God had given me the grace for the particular season I was in to complete my assignment. I was purpose-driven.

When you discover your purpose, you find your success. What will you do at all costs to reach your destiny? What is the purpose of the vision God has given you? What problem are you meant to solve?

As a kingdom entrepreneur, God has bestowed on me a gift that I apply to a business in which I can bring glory to Him and impact lives in the marketplace. We all have the opportunity to operate in excellence so that others can see the Spirit of God operating in and through us. Being able to stand in righteousness, showing love, and serving our clients, afford us the opportunity to be a catalyst for change. Entrepreneurship gives us the ability to influence others' lives. The biggest transformation is the person we become in the process. As we submit under the leadership of God, our walk, talk, and the way we think, change. Every step of obedience reveals more of the person God has destined us to become.

Let's get started and dig right in! The first step to unmasking purpose is to identify where you currently find yourself on your journey of discovery (The Purpose Map). This dictates where you are going. You may also find that you need to step out of your comfort zone. You cannot grow and be comfortable at the same time.

THE PURPOSE MAP

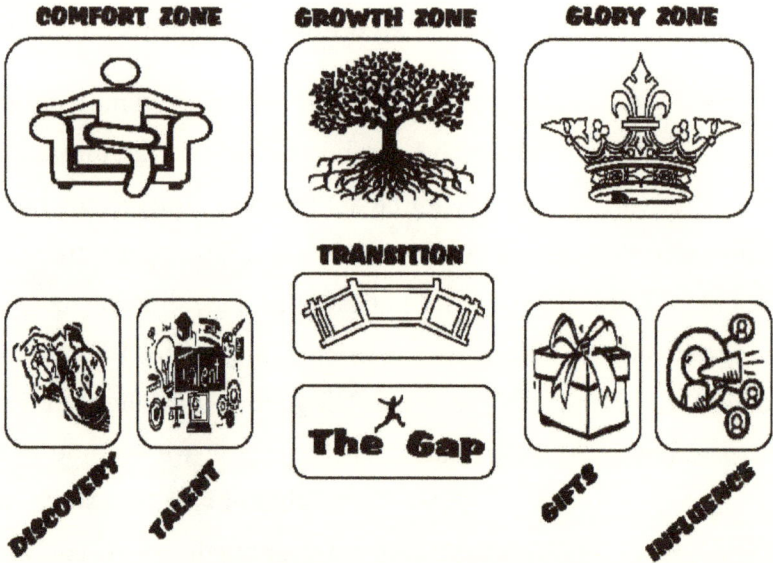

COMFORT ZONE (DISCOVERING SELF AND TALENTS)

Who Am I Supposed To Be?

I was never an avid fan of name calling or of labels given by spectators. We tend to label people with what they do. We need to be cautious about attaching words to who we are and our perceived identity. Words carry so much power that they can change the trajectory of someone's life. The propensity to label people may stem from traditional beliefs or perceptions. Tradition is a system of beliefs or actions that has been passed down from generation to generation. When one upholds old unbiblical traditions, even if they don't make sense or produce any results, it places people in bondage. Tainted traditional belief is one of the biggest sources of wrong thinking. It becomes a rule of thumb, a protocol, and part of the status quo for many people. Do not hold onto old cultural rules for fear of being judged and seen as different. When you are being your authentic-self and get a revelation of your divine identity, you will start challenging unbiblical traditions. Jesus was also judged because of tradition: it is written, "Can any good come out of Nazareth?"

At some point growing up during my teenage years, I believed the notion that boys were only attracted to girls with long hair and green eyes. Boy, was I wrong! I had to learn to embrace my imperfections and focus on the inner person God created rather than on my outward appearance. I am glad I made the decision to love God's masterpiece, which was all of me. He wants to make everything new and replace any broken beliefs you may have with blessed beliefs.

Another distorted belief that may be detrimental to your progress, is that you need a degree to be successful. When you discover your gifts, success finds you.

Let us go through some beliefs to unveil unruly thought patterns:

Belief 1 – Approval

As mentioned in a previous chapter, you do not need the approval of others to be loved. Your insecurities and low self-worth may keep you in isolation and prevent you from expressing your true self to the world. Some of you may believe that your views are not important and that you have nothing significant to contribute to others. How did the affirmations and approval from others shape your beliefs?

Belief 2 – Rejection

When you feel rejected because of your past, you think that others will reject you in future. Your relationships may have a short lifespan because of your built-in defence mechanisms that were developed over time. Someone else does not need to be victim of your past pain. Everyone faces rejection in their life, and no one is exempted. How do you respond to rejection? How did fear of failure shape your beliefs?

Belief 3 – Repeated Cycles

Certain behaviours and distorted beliefs may become bad habits. Do you find that you end up in unhealthy relationships time and time again? You fight the same battles and end up engulfed in shame and guilt, leaving your thinking unchanged. Often it is not something that you have done, but the iniquities that have been passed down through your generational line. What are the things you do simply because it has always been done that way? Is it in contradiction to the word of God?

It is vital to name the belief that has been misleading you if you want to see breakthrough and discover yourself. As you think, so you will become. Set time aside to complete the belief sheet, and work through it during your quiet time.

My Belief System

The enemy's primary weapon is deception as he fights the plan of God for your life. When you are deceived, you believe something that is not true. Although, it's not true, it appears to be true to you because that is what you believe. What false beliefs have you allowed to influence your thinking and values? What is it that you will have to unlearn and replace with the truth of God's word? This exercise will penetrate to the deepest part of your heart, and it will help renew your mind and engrave the truth. Action is key if you want to see breakthrough, so invest in yourself by completing the tasks, even if you have to come back to them again and again.

TASK 1

Belief	Who wrote or said it	Broken or Blessed

TASK 2

My mission statement in life is to_____

_____

Ask yourself these five questions:

1. What is my calling?
2. Who needs to hear my story?
3. Whom do I need to serve with my gifts?
4. What problem am I meant to solve?
5. Why did God choose me?

Summarise your overcomer story here in a few words with a motivation to help others.

_____

_____

_____

_____

_____

_____

GROWTH ZONE – THE GAP

What Is Happening To Me?

You were born to make a difference, not just to make a living. Every follower was born to be a leader of their gift, not only of people. God's plan was never for anyone to be a perpetual follower. We became followers when we lost our leadership spirit and separated ourselves from God. This is how you became a victim of your context and culture. You will face situations where you can make a difference if you have the courage and conviction to do so. You are an agent of change.

You are in the gap if you have outgrown your comfort zone. These questions will guide you into the next phase of your purpose-driven life:

- What season are you finding yourself in and what are the signs?

- What frustrations are you feeling that indicate that it's time to move onto the next season?

- What vision do you have that has been lying dormant?

- What unpleasant experiences have been holding you back from moving onto the next season?

- What has happened to you that you now realise was for the good?

There is a hidden treasure inside of you waiting to be unlocked. This is where you have to endure the process and allow God to refine you. You have to push yourself and eliminate any thoughts of giving up. A paradigm shift is about to take place on your road to destiny. Take a deep breath. You will fall in love with the person you are about to become.

Unlocking Hidden Treasures

Attributes:	
Skills & Abilities:	
Accomplishments or what you want to accomplish:	
Experiences:	

Talents:	
And more:	

Below are some guidance tools to implement in order to help you graduate to the glory or influential zone. Many get stuck in the gap zone because they fail to take action. You have to motivate and push yourself to get through this curve. Your future is on the other side. Everyone has twenty four hours in a day; how you use those hours is what makes all the difference to your life!

Guidance Tool 1

Write the vision down

A vision is something that you imagine or dream to achieve. Where there is no vision, people perish (Proverbs 29:18). You may have a vision to have your own feeding scheme. God places the desire inside of you and you initiate it by taking action. If you don't have a vision, you will have nothing to strive towards, and you will be pulled in all kinds of directions. You may find that you need to take a detour from where you currently invest your resources. First pray, and then plan. Hold yourself accountable every day. Get a vision board (see below) if you are more of a visual person, so that you can get a picture of who it is you want to become, then move backwards to the beginning of the process. Make a commitment not just to write down your vision but to follow through with it. Revise your vision after six months to see if you are on track to reach your goal, and if not, make the necessary changes.

Guidance Tool 2

Let go of the past

You cannot overcome what you are not willing to confront. You are not able to take everyone and all your old habits into your new season. There are some people you will have to leave behind. These individuals may not necessarily be bad people, but they may become stumbling blocks to you and prevent you from reaching your destiny. Separation is preparation for what lies ahead and emotions should not interfere with your decisions.

Guidance Tool 3

Confess what you want through scripture

You can quote scriptures that relate to what you are going through, until they stick and become a part of you. Place them on the wall, behind your mirror, and in your closet, so you can be reminded of them. Discipline and commitment will be key in your journey.

Guidance Tool 4

Invest in yourself

If it doesn't make you grow, let it go. Take care of your emotional, spiritual, mental, and physical health, and reach out to experts in the field if you have to. Put realistic goals and plans in place that set you up for your future growth. If God shows you the invisible (what is yet to be seen), the impossible becomes possible. Do not become stuck in this zone as many do. You have destiny calling your name. Keep on moving.

Create Your Own Vision Board

Choose to live a life of excellence and significance by making your own vision board. Planning is an important tool if you want to reach your goal. If you have a goal without an action plan you will not achieve the outcome you have set out to achieve. The purpose of the vision board is to bring everything together. It serves as a reminder of where you see yourself moving towards. It is a life-changing guide towards your future. The goal you set must be relevant to your purpose and to the stage you find yourself in life. Many have opted for resolutions that are merely words and ideas. Do you know of anyone who took action on their New Year Resolutions? Vision boards help you see the bigger picture and what your life can become when you are focused on achieving your goals. It is more than a random collection of words and images.

Here are a few simple guidelines to help you on your journey:

Use your imagination and start brainstorming

You need to sit down and start thinking what it is you really want in life. It can include finances, health, personal development, business, your family, ministry, mental and emotional well-being, and/or your self-worth goals. Be honest with yourself, and jot down your desires. If you want to lose weight, write it down. If you want to get rid of bad habits, write it down. Don't be too concerned about how you will attain it, just write it down. The key is to put your thoughts on paper.

Set realistic goals

Once you are done brainstorming, ask yourself where you want to be a year from now, and set goals towards that. Write down five goals for every area you mentioned, and put realistic timelines to them. Start with the goals that are priorities to you, and work your way down the list. For example, if you want to start a business and make a profit in one year, and you haven't started planning yet, this goal may not be too realistic. You can make it part of your three to five year vision in order to make it attainable. A fun element could be to celebrate your success, no matter how insignificant it appears to be.

The 'Smarter' Acronym will equip you to measure and set the right goals in place:

Specific **M**easurable **A**ttainable

Risky (have to be dedicated to go for it) **T**imeline with a date (hold yourself accountable) **E**xciting (fun element)

Relevant to your purpose

Craft your vision through words and images

Pictures are going to be the basis of your vision board, so you can include photos from travel magazines or whatever interests you. Select images based on what you want to see in the future, and arrange them on the board in a design that you love. They must be authentic and should speak volumes about your personality. You can include family pictures, where you would like to travel etc. This is a creative space to attach your dreams to your vision board, and it can also be used in conjunction with your declarations for victory, if you have any doubts about achieving the vision. Remove the limits of your thinking, and stretch yourself.

Speak life by affirming it with words

This is the space to include words and motivational phrases of who you want to become. There is only room for positivity and dream activations in this area, so go all out. If you aspire to be wealthy and healthy, make it your declaration. You can use words like 'I am loved' and 'I can be whomever I decide to be'. If you want to see the change, this is the birthing place of your dreams. Be true to your convictions and feelings of wanting to be successful.

Action speaks louder than words

Now you have to place your vision board in a place where you will see it every day, so that it can motivate you. It can be next to your mirror or on your door – wherever it stands out. Make it a daily exercise to look at it. You can review it before you go to bed, or first thing when you wake up in the morning. As you attain your dreams and goals, remember to tick them off, and continue to set new ones for yourself. Celebrate the small victories with friends and family. Having an attitude of gratitude and thankfulness makes room to receive more. And remember, if you can see it, you can achieve it. If you skipped a few days, go back and start again. Come back to the guidelines and tasks that you set for yourself, even if you have to repeat it again. Don't procrastinate; it's not only a thief of time but a thief of life!

GLORY ZONE (GIFTS AND INFLUENCE)

How Did God Design Me?

How you think, see your problems, perceive things, and your desire to help others, all reveal your design. Your God-given Purpose Strategy (GPS) relates to your struggles in life and how well you use them to push you into your destiny. When you unlock your unique built-in strategy, doors will open that no man can shut. Whenever you do something that you have never done before, you might discover something that you never knew you had to start with. Your God-given gifts are meant to serve others and improve their lives. Marshawn Daniels wrote, *Gifts are things we are called to do, not just things we can do. The individuals that are impacted the most by your gifts have acknowledged and received it.*

I love the following verses from the King James Version of the Bible on gifts:

A gift is a precious stone in the eyes of him that hath it: whithersoever it turneth, it prospereth. Proverbs 17:8 (KJV)

A man's gift maketh room for him, and bringeth him before great men.

Proverbs 18:16 KJV

Giving is an important etiquette in the Middle Eastern culture. If you do not present a gift, they will not do business with you. By demonstrating good manners and respect for the cultural practices, you gain favour with great men. Seek revelation for the value of your gift. Pray over your gift. Your gift or present will open up doors of opportunity for you. The 'gift spot' is activated when something you do brings you great joy, comes naturally to you, and ignites your passion. For instance, my own gifts are analysing, encouraging, mentoring, strategizing, networking and giving.

Answer Your Why?

Who do you want to help and why?

What is important to you?

What cause are you fighting for?

What life lesson or principle do you want to be known for?

Your gift transcends to a new level the moment you serve others with it. You might possess the same or more. A talent for me might be a gift for you. Your strength could be my weakness, depending on how we are wired, and vice versa. You may not know your gift instantaneously because you haven't fully explored and developed it yet. Your gift means nothing if it is not supported by good character and integrity. Character is when your words, your deeds, and your actions are one. It means sacrificing for principles even if it means losing friends. Character is integrity, meaning that you are integrated, or one, with yourself.

The more you venture from the norm to unfamiliar territory, the more your gift will stand out. You have to try it before you decline it. In hindsight, I have always had the characteristics of a leader. In Grade R, I would speak out when I was told to remain quiet, and I always dared to be different. I loved initiating tasks and being a trailblazer. I acquired a resilience over the years, motivating others to step out of their comfort zones and to push the limitations of what people say they could not become. It's a burning passion inside of me that fuels my purpose. Your passion also will separate you from everyone else.

Your *gift* could be:

Giving

Drawing

Communicating

Teaching

Creating

Encouraging

Caretaking

Cooking

Designing

Writing

Organising

Advising

Strategizing

Hospitality

Managing

Make a list and write down what your God-given gifts are. As you identify them, you will require more self-confidence to operate in those gifts and to influence those around you.

God-Confidence

When you fail to have confidence in yourself, you fail to have confidence in the God who made you. When you choose to be bold and do something regardless of how you feel, you are making a declaration and waging war on the enemy. If you want to be used by God, you will need to have God-confidence – confidence in Christ's power and ability to work in and through you. Whenever doubt torments your mind, if you want to win the battle you will need to speak out the word of God. When you do not believe, you live in doubt and unbelief, which is contrary to the word of God. Double-mindedness does not please God. The significance behind David's slaying his giant Goliath was that he had confidence in God to fight the battle for him. You may be the least likely to succeed in your circle of friends, but your belief in God will catapult you towards being a giant slayer. Refuse to believe only in your own capabilities, and go forth in God's ability. To have courage is not the absence of fear, but to have the tenacity and supernatural strength for a God-given assignment, with or without fear.

The difference between gifts and talents are outlined below: Source: Marshawn Daniels

Talents	Gifts
Comfort zone	Glory Zone
What we've learned to do	What we're called to do
Formed Identity	Born Identity
The Rules (Protocol)	Glory (Higher purpose)
Decided	Imparted
Doing	Being
Driven (Achievement)	Directed (Alignment)
Grinding and striving	Grace and surrender
Fight	Flow
Trying	Teaching
Task-driven	Testimony-driven
Super-skills	Superpowers
Discipline	Destiny
Mountain climbing	Miracle unleashing
Success and safety	Significance
Labels and titles	Lessons and transformation
Muscle	The message
Student	Teacher

Your Voice Matters

Being a voice to the voiceless brings significance. Not everyone is called to be a preacher; some are message-carriers, story tellers, life changers, or gift givers. Be intentional about finding ways to share your message with the right audience who carry your spiritual DNA and have been waiting for you to manifest yourself to the rest of the world. As you influence society and impact nations with your gift, take a pause to assess whether you are on the right path before continuing. Always leave room for growth and remember what God has taken you out of. Break the silence of addiction and be fearless in speaking your truth. Speak up for what is right and be a Kingdom ambassador for Christ. You are being deployed with a heavenly mandate. The more you move, the more you increase your capacity.

When Jesus was tempted in the wilderness He knew His assignment and what He was called to. His response was always backed with the living word which nullified all false accusations. The reason the enemy is wiping out this generation is because they do not fully understand their Kingdom mandate and God-given purpose.

Your life-defying moments that almost destroyed you brought you here. It required an open heart, a teachable spirit, and an appetite for more. You are unstoppable and a force to be reckoned with, and you have an agility to turn your setbacks into comebacks when you have been released from the bondage of negative cultural beliefs. Do not be afraid to tell your story. If you don't, you may deny someone else the opportunity of being set free and sharing their story. Give yourself permission to break free from a generation of oppression: write that book, be a problem solver. Your convictions are greater than your biggest fears. You just don't know it yet. Failure is not the lack of accomplishing a goal, it is when you have a goal and you don't pursue it. Find yourself a spiritual mentor or peer coach to guide and pray you into your next season. In a business sphere, the mentor can even be younger than you, or anyone who has obtained the success and expertise you are aspiring to.

Ivy Mc Gregor, a global influencer, once said, "You need ones, twos and threes in your life. Do not be too heavy with the twos and balance them out with ones and threes. Learn to position people in your life and choose them well."

Ones are your mentors – people who have been where you want to be.

Twos are contemporaries – your friends, colleagues etc.

Threes are your mentees – those that look up to you.

And remember, it is essential to your growth to be surrounded by successful individuals who have achieved what you are currently striving for. In a business sphere, listen to absorb their success stories, and apply the pearls of wisdom to your own life.

Keys to Unlock your God-given Purpose Strategy (GPS)

In aviation, the pilot has to decide on a destination before he or she is allowed to proceed with take-off. There are certain pre-flight checks that need to be adhered to before the aircraft is allowed to be airborne. The pilot will never leave the ground without his or her flight plan. The Air Traffic Control (ATC) tower instructs the pilot where to fly, because they see the total picture. The tower knows where the aircrafts are located in the vicinity. They guide the pilot to fly fast, or to slow down, so the pilot doesn't end up crashing into another aircraft. In the same manner, God knows where every detour is located around you. Never take instructions from other pilots who have their own flight plan to follow. Only follow the guidance of the tower, which is the Holy Spirit. When He instructs us to change our course to avoid a catastrophic incident, then that is what we must do. When you encounter unexpected disruptions in your life, take a detour, but keep moving towards your destination. A detour, or change of course, can appear between any of the phases illustrated in the blueprint below. Eliminate the gaps before moving onto the next step. You cannot answer your why if you have not written the vision down. You will struggle to activate your gifts if you do not have a relationship with the Holy Spirit. Be sure to remove all the stumbling blocks when unveiling purpose. Invest your time and resources in the things pulling you towards destiny. If you are an aspiring entrepreneur, here are some winning strategies to unlock your hidden potential:

Ten Kingdom Keys for Aspiring Entrepreneurs

1. Spend time in God's presence before brainstorming. Set the atmosphere, make a decision to commit, and then follow through, whatever it takes. Get an idea of what it is you want to do, and work on your logo, brand colours, vision, clear goals etc. Whom have you told about the business idea? Who is the person in your life that

reminds you of your goals? We all need that one person in life who will not let us quit. Find someone who can hold you accountable and help you to go from having a great business idea to being an entrepreneur that impacts others' lives. Your business idea is like a seed. Nurture it, water it, and pray over it. Be a good steward of the vision God gave you.

2. Write down your vision/idea, and revisit it as often as you can because it will keep changing. It may present itself as keywords, pictures, prophecy, spoken words, or dreams. God speaks through whom He sees fit to get a message through to you. Has a random person ever approached you and suggested that you start your own business? I'm sure you can relate. The enemy does not have the ability to place desires and ideas in our hearts to prosper. So it can only be God.

3. Use your vision board, and dream it into existence. Think of the desired outcome and end goal when planning, then work your way back to the beginning. When vision and passion meet, you are unstoppable. Be innovative. Everyone is an accountant or a manager, so you have to become an expert in your industry and introduce yourself as a 'specialist' or 'master' to describe your trade, e.g. 'master in finance' has a greater appeal than 'financial manager'. Ensure you have done proper research, and use every opportunity to upgrade your skills.

4. Take small actions daily to establish new habits. Focus on renewing your mind to enter the next level of leadership, and you will achieve the goals as the by-product. (Romans 12:2). Have an 'inside-out' approach.

5. Register the business, then download the simple steps online and a template of a business plan. Get a coach, a fellow entrepreneur, or someone with knowledge in your field to assist with the set up process. Invest in your development (learn how to sell online, learn about marketing on social media, attend a workshop, virtual meetings, free masterclass etc.). Initially, you may not have to leave your job to start your entrepreneurship journey, depending on the nature of the business you want to start. You will know when the business needs you to be there full-time. The purpose is to start somewhere, and bring your vision to life. Be willing to take risks.

6. Get yourself a landing page (one-page website) to market your services. Pray for a divine strategy to meet the right people who will invest in your dream, and for a plan to obtain the required finances. If you have a background in administration and accounts, it will ease the process; if not, invest in a bookkeeper, or someone to manage the administrative duties. After the pandemic, many businesses may make use of virtual assistants per hour, so do your homework on what will be cost effective for you. Network every opportunity you get, and start working on growing your personal brand.

There is power in who you associate yourself with. If God ordained it, He will make provision for it.

7. Identify whether you want to sell a product or a service, and what it will do for your potential client. Are you confident in your product? Do your research; study the possible objections potential clients may have before you sell to them.

8. Identify the specific target market you will cater for. If you sell to all, you sell to none. For instance, are you planning to provide for business coaches in your suburb or city? Your target market may be an industry, or it may be a specialised field. Ensure they are able to pay for the product/services you can offer. Identify what needs you are meeting. What are your clients' biggest PAIN POINTS?

9. What value are you giving to your ideal client? Who are your competitors, and where are they failing to deliver? What can you offer that your competitors can't match? You will have to give a few things for free, and also add value so that your potential clients will want to buy from you.

10. Identify your 'help statement' for the purpose of your business before launching.

I help _____ so that they can _____ without_. _____

For instance, I help **young professionals** so that they can **discover their purpose** without **wasting years of their life unfulfilled.**

Use your 'I help' statement on social media platforms and when introducing yourself to potential clients and partners. You have one minute to make a good impression. Announce the launch of your business on all social media platforms once you have implemented the necessary steps above.

Blueprint for your God-given purpose strategy (GPS)

Apply the tools for overcoming addiction →Apply tools for inner healing → Write your Vision → Write the Goals → What are your Values → Commit to taking ACTION → Identify your zone on the purpose map → Locate where you are and what you are striving towards → Have a clear understanding of how your pain serves a purpose → Replace broken beliefs with blessed ones→ Re-assess if your environment is conducive for fulfilling your purpose→ Formulate your Mission Statement → Identify your talents → Identify your gifts → Answer your why?→ Know your calling → Know who you are called to → Understand your kingdom assignment → Remove destiny killers → Pray for destiny helpers→ Define what success looks like to you→ Formulate an action plan → Be intentional about pursuing purpose → Prioritise your tasks/time in alignment with your purpose.

You are well on your way to discovering purpose. You just have to start. The key ingredient is to take action. You will figure the rest out along the way. When you write your vision down, you are giving God permission to act on your behalf. He has designed you to attract abundance in every sphere you influence. You are influencing your future when you come into agreement with God's promises.

Chapter Thirteen

GOD IS THE AUTHOR OF YOUR STORY

As for us, we have all of these great witnesses who encircle the clouds. So we must let go of every wound that has pierced us and the sin we so easily fall into. Then we will be able to run life's marathon race with passion and determination, for the path has been already marked out before us. Hebrew 12:1 (TPT)

You are not the addictions you are/were enslaved to, nor are you the culmination of your bad choices in life. You were not created to survive but to thrive. There is a path waiting to be discovered that leads to your destiny. It is not a straight road and has many obstacles along the way, but be of good courage because God has placed destiny helpers all around you. Your destiny helpers carry the same spiritual DNA as you and have been assigned to your life to help you walk out your purpose. Your story is the sum of your life experiences. Your calling connects you to the needs of this generation, of your community, and of the neighbourhood you live in. God yearns for you to fulfil your purpose.

Your path and your struggles may be different from mine, but our battle scars connect us. The common denominator is that God is the author of our story. If you are not called to some arena of ministry or public service, perhaps you are a mother raising a child of destiny in that arena. You have a heavenly mandate to restore a broken generation. The Kingdom of God is about resurrection power; it is not only a form of godliness and religious gatherings. Being in church your whole life is no proof that the church has been in you.

When you do not become whole as an individual the outcomes are 'bleeding' families and communities. What are you willing to build to prevent this from happening in the future?

Your testimony carries the power to set others free. If you have overcome a drug addiction, write your victory statement on paper, and host a workshop on how you became free. If you are a millennial who struggled with secret sin and your parents are pastors, be the first to remove any labels others have put on you. Stand up, child of purpose, and hold your head up high. You are not judged by the achievements of your parents. You are walking out your own unique purpose, and your story needs to be heard. We are all imperfect beings serving a perfect God.

There is power in association and the circle of friends you allow to speak into your life. If you are surrounded by barren people who are not good for you, who are hindering your growth, or who are choking your destiny and ability to succeed, ask God to remove them. The reason they are clinging to you may be because they have given up on their dreams, and are living in regret, and looking for company to soothe the pain and wounds they refuse to be healed from. God wants you free from self-sabotage, insecurities, suicidal thoughts, approval addiction, rejection, shame, and guilt.

During the outbreak of the global pandemic we entered 'The Great Spiritual Awakening' in which God allowed us to be in lockdown in order to spend time with Him and answer our 'why'. At the time of writing this chapter, we are on level 3 of the lockdown in South Africa, amidst the global corona virus pandemic. The Covid-19 death toll in South Africa on day 114 of the lockdown since the beginning of the total shutdown was 4 948, with Gauteng (128 604) reported to be highest in numbers in positive cases identified, followed by the Western Cape (85 411). Many lives have been claimed since the outbreak of the virus, and it has left families mourning for their loved ones. It affected everyone, whether directly or indirectly. I recently learned of the passing of a few friends' parents, and a colleague's spouse, who lost their battle to the virus. The fear and uncertainty is tangible as the world is adapting to the new normal. Public handshakes and hugging are a thing of the past, and are replaced with 'elbow greeting' to assist in flattening the curve. It has also led to isolation and avoiding close contact with people, which impacts emotional and mental health.

The world as we know it is adapting to change, and many believe it will not return to 'business as usual' when lockdown is lifted. We are living in times in which our reliance on God will make us stand out. When we give Him our "yes" He graces us for the next season. His love for us is unconditional and has no end. It is in the light of these devastating events that purpose is unmasked and potential unlocked to maximise our time left on this earth.

Life after our global crisis is not going to become easier as the stresses of life show up at our doorsteps, attempt to reside with us, and want to dictate to us. Crisis is a human condition, an event we have no control over, but it is not necessarily permanent; we can hope that we are experiencing temporary discomfort and that, like other crises', this one too shall pass. Whatever the outcome of this crisis, born again believers are given an opportunity to apply their faith when everyone else is shaken by fear and anxiety. Kingdom influencers find a solution for every problem amidst challenges, and are not defeated. We are the salt and the light of this world. The word of God is a light unto our path and a beacon of hope to the lost in a dark world.

During my Safety and Emergency Procedures Training (SEPT), our theoretical and practical assessments were done annually before our aircraft ratings expiredin order to remain currentinline with CivilAviation Regulation Standards (CARS). Thereafter, every three years we were retrained in order to remain competent as flight crew. For some strange reason, I was always eager to partake in these assessments. They entailed being placed in a pitch dark simulator, and wearing a heavy smoke hood and protective breathing equipment that incorporated an oxygen system, to prevent the wearer from inhaling smoke gases in a smoke-filled environment. We were tasked with finding the closest exit during a 'mock up' emergency evacuation. In a real life-threatening situation there could be debris, smoke, gases, possibly a raging fire, and unforeseen obstacles. The chances of survival after smoke inhalation are less than having a fire in the aircraft. In the test scenario, I was paired with a fellow crew member. We had to assist one another and follow the instructions of the examiner. To add 'fuel to the fire', the room was filled with simulated smoke. After putting on your smoke hood while in a seated position, you then stand in the upright position and turn a few times before the assessment commences. This leaves you disorientated for a brief moment.

We had it all figured out. We worked out our 'life strategy' by counting the chairs and jumping over 'pretend dead bodies' that posed a threat. The moment the examiner gave the go ahead, the adrenaline started kicking in. Even during the darkest moment, we are alerted to any danger ahead and we need to act. We have to envision the light at the end of the tunnel before us. I started counting, and used the chairs to guide me. My colleague was right next to me as we shouted our made-up commands, "First row", "Second row", "Third row", "We're almost there" and "One more row." Then we take a sharp left and bang on the steel door to alert the examiner that we have completed the assessment. Suddenly light floods the dark room, and we can finally see and breathe again! The simulator became familiar territory, so we completed the assessment faster each time. Seconds can feel like minutes, and minutes can feel like hours. It required a team effort.

Some of the flight attendants who had been flying for twenty years would panic and become anxious before they began, because of the lack of strategy. If you failed the practical scenario, you had to do it again before moving onto the next practical assessment – 'raft management' in aviation terms – which prepares the learner in the event of a 'ditching' (water landing). This one has a one percent survival rate. Bring it on!

Needless to say, experience is not always a good indicator that you have it all figured out. Our minds have the ability to trick us into thinking we will fail before we even get started. In real life, it is during these times that we should keep moving, and follow the still small voice of the Holy Spirit.

God brings the word, which is a lamp to our feet, to remembrance when we need it the most. In the dark, you do not know where to step, or do not even have the ability to move forward. Darkness cannot persist in light that shows a clear pathway. If there were no darkness, would we need God's light? If the light of God had failed to pull me out of my addictions, I could not testify and allow my light to break forth for someone else. It is comforting to know that God is always with us and has already prepared the way for us. God has not called us to walk this road alone, but to do His work within a community of people.

I have shared my story of redeeming love with you, the reader, and now it's up to you to give God permission to co-write yours. God is incomprehensible, and no words can do justice in describing Him. He sent His one and only Son to die on the cross for you, so you can walk in victory and no longer be a slave to your sin and addiction.

The more time you spend in the presence of God, the more you will know who you are. He is your Creator and you were created in His image. Before sin came in and separated us from God, His original intention for our lives was to desire, worship, and glorify Him in the earth. You may be stuck in the middle of a maze. You may have been stagnant for many years, not able to let go of the past. Perhaps you are searching for answers. Perhaps you keep arriving at a dead end, or perhaps you merely have a strong desire to change and are tired of fighting with yourself. You may be a parent of a child with an addiction, and you have reached the end of the road. You may have tried it your way, and it showed no results. Don't stop praying. God wants to give you an eternal promise for a temporary problem. Keep on pushing. Be intentional about the words that you speak, because there is life and death in the power of the tongue (Proverbs 18:21). Words spoken in frustration will produce the fruit of frustration. Words spoken with faith will produce the fruit of faith. Keep on shining your light, and remain in Him.

I speak life into your dead situation in the mighty name of Jesus. When you admit that you are broken, God begins to move. He can only do a transformational work with what you surrender to Him. Your brokenness serves a purpose that allows God to turn into good what the enemy meant for harm. I am praying for you. The world needs you. The woman attempting to commit suicide is waiting for your testimony. You are more powerful than you think.

You might not be where you want to be, but you are well on your way. Your identity precedes your actions, and before there was any sin, God had already accepted you. He removed your sins as far as the east is from the west. Many who have been walking this journey for years are held back by regret and still don't know their purpose. Don't be one of them.

You want more, and there is more. God has written the script for you and longs to be a part of every scene as you act your part in His story. I remember watching a Joyce Meyer DVD series on 'Battlefield of the Mind' leading up to my encounter with God. At the end of every podcast there would be an invitation to accept Jesus Christ as Lord and Saviour. I was wrestling with the idea, filled with the conviction from the Holy Spirit, so I switched off the television whenever it came to that part. You might be experiencing that right now, weighing what you will have to give up to fully surrender. God loves you so much that He pursues you no matter how many times you decline the gift of salvation. He is a real gentleman and has given us free will. If you are battling with fear, the feeling of fear may remain but that doesn't mean that you cannot do it afraid. It is a life-changing decision, not a feeling. If God had to wait until you were ready, there would be no need for grace. He deliberately chooses you based on your struggles and weaknesses, lest you boast and take all the glory for what He will accomplish through you.

God wants to give you the keys (authority) of the Kingdom of heaven. It may be that the foundation that you have built your life on is shaking. Jesus wants to rebuild what has been broken. He is the permanent solution to a temporary experience. You don't have to run away from God. Instead run into His loving arms that have been waiting for you all this time. God will never abandon you. If you sense that you have to recommit your life to the Lord after drifting away from His love, you can rededicate it to Him.

Repeat the prayer of salvation after me:

Heavenly Father, I repent for being outside of your will. Please forgive me for all of my sins. I believe you sent your one and only Son, Jesus Christ who was crucified on the cross, was buried, and rose again on the third day. I receive you into my heart and confess that Jesus is my Lord and Saviour. Please fill me with your Holy Spirit. I am saved, I am now a child of God and I surrender my life to you. In the name of Jesus, I pray. Amen.

If you read that prayer, and sincerely believed every word, then you are child of God, ready to be equipped to leave a legacy for your future generations. Be sure to join a local Bible-based church for water baptism, and for fellowship as you grow in Him. The water baptism is a public declaration of the decision you have made. It follows the example that Jesus Christ set before you when He was baptised by John the Baptist. When you are submerged under the water you leave your old self behind and come up as a new creation. *Or don't you know that all of us who were baptised into Christ Jesus were baptised into His death? We were therefore buried with Him through baptism into death in order that as Christ was raised from the dead through the glory of the Father, we too may live a new life.* (Romans 6:3-4, NIV)

It is important that you listen to sound doctrine and teachings, and that you learn to follow the promptings of the Holy Spirit. Join a community of believers to fellowship with, so that you can grow spiritually and be led by the Holy Spirit at all times. The word of God is your manual for life, so be sure to spend time reading it. And spread the good news that Jesus is the Jewish Messiah who came to establish God's Kingdom on earth. His sacrifice was for more than the Jews; it was for the whole world.

If you have already devoted your life to the Lordship of Jesus Christ,

then put on the full armour of God: put on your helmet of salvation to protect your head (thoughts), girdle the buckle of truth around your waist, with the breastplate of righteousness, shield of faith, have your feet fitted and ready with the gospel of peace, and overthrow darkness with the Sword of the Spirit which is the word of God. Be sober and alert at all times as you make your requests known to God in prayer. The weapons of warfare are not against the flesh but against the dark forces, cosmic powers, principalities, and spiritual forces of wickedness in the heavenly places. (Ephesians 6:10-

20) You have been deployed with a heavenly mandate to be a light carrier and a giant slayer in your generation.

As your love story with God unfolds, you will see that He has always been there, from day one, pursuing you, and waiting to write your story with you. Your life struggle was your unique God-given Purpose Strategy (GPS) after all. The love of God will never take you where the grace of God will not keep you. You are a generational curse breaker: a 'person committed to building legacy by breaking the cycle of emotional, mental, and financial poverty that previously plagued your lineage'. Look back at your generations, and you will see how God's story weaves its way through history, revealing redemption as He rescues people for Himself. Your story intertwines with your generation's story, and is knit into God's story.

And now...................

After being faced with retrenchment in the midst of a crisis, God spoke and I listened. I knew the right time would come for me to move on to my greater calling, and to spread my wings in a world with endless opportunities. There is a great purpose to the detour that God is taking me on. I made the decision to 'hang up my wings' and enter another chapter of my life. Before I joined the airline, I was a girl with a dream, and now I am exiting as a resilient woman with a vision, walking confidently in her purpose. I grew into a woman during my time with the airline that presented me with many opportunities. I love networking, and I met some of the most amazing people during my flights on and off the aircraft.

Flying can be a toxic environment for anyone struggling with addictions. You have free rein in countries with different area codes and foreign faces, and you have the freedom to let all your inhibitions go. A 'debriefing' is a gathering/party that would occur in a designated crew room during our layover at any destination. If you ask any flight attendant about it, they will deny it. So let's keep this between me and you! At the beginning of my flying career I literally crawled from pub to pub with fellow colleagues: from Red Cat underground club in Frankfurt to club hopping in Leicester Square, London, often ending up walking back to the hotel barefoot.

Then God stepped in and transformed my life. During the latter seven years the 'debriefings' changed to divinely appointed meetings with the amazing crew I flew with. I started guiding them towards their destiny and became more intentional when speaking into their lives. Whether it was in the foyer of the hotel in New York, the breakfast table in Sao Paulo, the poolside in Accra, sitting on a service bin in the middle of the night during our shifts, or while commuting to work from Cape Town to Johannesburg, I was positioned for a purpose.

Soaring the skies will always be a part of me. I will treasure the excursions in Ghana at the local market sourcing colourful fabrics while walking in the scorching sun close to fainting; roaming the streets of Mainz and stuffing my face with their famous schnitzels; exploring the streets of Time Square in New York; having 'counselling sessions' in the galley on our crew jumpseats; sitting on service bins in the middle of the night sharing our life stories; being chased by the locals while negotiating low prices at

the night markets in Hong Kong; the lively atmosphere in Sao Paulo when walking in the streets; meeting beautiful souls on my flights and randomly exchanging stories; praying for nervous flyers while they squeeze my hand until it loses its colour; serving guests with the warmest African hospitality thirty six thousand feet above sea level; and surprising honeymoon couples with a glass of bubbly on their way to Mauritius.

The fourteen years has been phenomenal and flying will always be a part of me. Who knows, my next mission trip may just end up taking me to familiar terrain. One thing is for sure, I will think twice before pressing the call bell, and will always remember to smile when served by a fellow crew member, because I know the sacrifices that come with it. When I hear the words "chicken or beef", it will have a whole new meaning, and I will be reminded of the promises of God.

Abraham obeyed God and left his homeland for a place where he had never been before. The Lord blessed him beyond measure, and he became the Father of many nations. Deborah arose at a time when women were not supposed to be on the front line. Barak refused to leave her behind, and she ended up leading the children of Israel into victory against their enemies.

The time has come to dream bigger, to be bolder, and to put on my armour as I slay giants for God. Destiny is whispering my name, and I am following the voice of God, expectant about where He will lead me. The wind is changing direction. I may not know where it's taking me to, but I trust Him completely.

What false sense of security are you clinging to? Are you at the place you are supposed to be at? Are you unfulfilled and tired of your employer determining your worth? Perhaps it's time to step out of your comfort zone and follow your passions. God is about to flip the switch in your life, as He starves your need for acceptance, pulls you out of your depression, changes your career path, and gives you a new heart.

You may not have the full revelation of what God is busy doing in your life, but God has confidence in you to create it, build it, and run with it, as you bring glory to His name. A trailblazer does not follow a path, but leaves his or her own trail behind. He or she is someone who is considered a first in their area or field of expertise. Trailblazers have a vision for a different future, a faith that turns their dreams into reality, and a determination that cuts through barriers and obstacles. You are about to encounter God like never before and change history. Believe it. Receive it.

VICTORY DECLARATIONS

In order to help you win, below is a list of scripture-based victory declarations and the different attributes of God. The wisdom confessions and meditations will reveal the abundant life promised to you.

Declarations for Victory over Addictions

In Jesus Name, I confess that:

I am complete in Christ.

I am delivered from the power of darkness.

I am protected by the blood of Jesus Christ.

I am called to set the captives free.

I am kept and saved by grace.

I am a disciple of Christ.

I am the salt of the earth.

I am born for greatness.

I am justified by faith.

I am a joint heir with Christ.

I am an ambassador for Christ, the light of the world.

I am a citizen of the kingdom of heaven.

I am redeemed by His love.

I am more than an overcomer in Jesus Christ.

I have the mind of Christ.

I am called to set the captives free.

I am delivered from the power of darkness.

I am chosen.

I am a citizen of the kingdom of heaven.

I belong to a royal priesthood.

I am complete in Christ.

I am blessed.

I am redeemed by His blood.

I walk in the Spirit and not in the flesh.

I am taking every thought captive to the obedience of Christ.

I am a co-labourer and heir of Christ.

I am fearfully and wonderfully made.

I am created in the image of God.

I am forgiven for all my sins.

I am healed in my mind body, spirit and soul.

I am a conqueror.

I am God's representative in the earth realm.

I have a unique gift and desire more.

I am born of incorruptible seed.

I am now a new creation in Christ.

I am not defined by my addictions and past mistakes.

I am Spirit filled and am not led by my emotions.

I will live and not die.

I speak life into dry bones and dead things.

I am not a slave of sin.

I have dominion in the earth.

The Nature of God (Who Is He to You?)

He is our Provider.

He is Eternal.

He is our Redeemer.

He is our Saviour.

He is a Covenant Keeper.

He is the God of more than enough.

He is a forgiving God.

He is the Beginning and the End.

He is our Healer.

He is Faithful.

He gives Eternal life.

He is Dependable.

He is Steadfast.

He is Always on time.

He is our Creator.

He restores us.

He is Sovereign.

He is sitting at the right hand of the Father.

He is Gracious.

He is Light in the darkness.

He is Merciful.

He is Unchanging.

He is a Miracle working God.

He is a Promise keeper.

He is our Abba Father.

He is Omniscient.

He is All-knowing.

He is Holy.

He is Righteous.

He is a Deliverer.

He is Love.

He is not a man that

He should lie.

He is the Truth.

He is our Source.

He is our Vindicator.

He is the Word.

He is I AM.

He is the King of Glory.

He is the Way.

He is Alive!

Jehovah Nissi – Our Victory.

Jehovah Shalom – Our Peace.

Jehovah Roi – The God who sees.

Jehovah Rapha – Our Healer.

Jehovah Jireh – Our Provider.

Personal commitment:

I hereby commit to praying for my destiny helpers and accountability partners every day, and to praying over my gifts. This is my declaration.

Prayer:

Lord, give those who need to release my blessing, ears to hear You, and a heart of obedience. Every element of this day, month, and year, will work in my favour; my destiny helpers will find me, and no good thing will be withheld from me today, in Jesus Name.

This is my decree for today; it will be established, and light shall shine on my path, in Jesus Name. Amen.

WISDOM DECLARATIONS:

Proverbs 2:10, 11

I decree and declare that discretion shall watch over me, and understanding shall keep me. I decree and declare that skilfulness and wisdom shall enter into my heart, knowledge shall be pleasant to me. I decree and declare that I will not turn aside to the right or to the left, and that I will keep my eyes focused on my purpose.

Proverbs 3:3

I decree and declare that mercy, kindness, and truth will not forsake me, that I will bind them around my neck and write them upon them tablet of my heart.

WISDOM SCRIPTURE MEDITATIONS:

Proverbs 3:5

Trust in the Lord with all your heart and lean not on your own understanding; in all your ways submit to him, and he will make your paths straight. Do not be wise in your own eyes; fear the Lord and shun evil.

Proverbs 4:23

Above all else, guard your heart, for everything you do flows from it.

Proverbs 7:2

Keep my commands and you will live; guard my teachings as the apple of your eye. Bind them on your fingers; write them on the tablet of your heart.

Proverbs 8:11

...for wisdom is more precious than rubies, and nothing you desire can compare with her. I, wisdom, dwell together with prudence; I possess knowledge and discretion.

Proverbs 8:30

Then I was constantly at his side. I was filled with delight day after day, rejoicing always in his presence

Proverbs 9:10

The fear of the Lord is the beginning of wisdom, and knowledge of the Holy One is understanding.

Proverbs 10:14

The wise store up knowledge, but the mouth of a fool invites ruin.

Proverbs 10:19

Sin is not ended by multiplying words, but the prudent hold their tongues.

Proverbs 10:32

The lips of the righteous know what finds favour, but the mouth of the wicked only what is perverse.

I stand in agreement with you, the reader, that the generational curse is broken, and I speak a generational blessing over your family:

May the Lord bless you
And keep you
Make His face shine upon you
The Lord turn His face towards you
And give you peace.
May His favour be upon you
Your family and your children
And their children, and their children
To a thousand generations............

ENDNOTES

INTRODUCTION

David, E. & Abdelmalek, M. 2020. Why scientists think COVID-19 may be spread through particles in the air. https://abcnews.go.com/USscientists- covid-19-spread-particles-air/story?=71665634 [8 July 2020].

CHAPTER TWO

Welton, J. 2012. Eyes of Honour. Training for Purity & Righteousness. Shippensburg, PA. Destiny Image.

Eckhardt, J. 2016. Fasting For Breakthrough and Deliverance. Lake Mary. Charisma House.

Covenant Eyes Ministry. 2020. Ministry of Tech, Technology advise and solutions. https://ministryoftech.com.au/covenanteyes/ [21 August 2020]. Like the Master Ministries. 2020. Porneia Definition – What is the meaning of the Greek word porneia in the Bible? https://derefmail.com/mail/ client/WO_ezq5Mb78/dereferrer/?redirectUrl=https%3A%2F%2F www. neverthirsty.org%2Fbible-qa%2Fqa-archives%2Fquestion%2Fwhat-is- meaning-of-greek-word-porneia-in-bible [21 August 2020].

CHAPTER 11

Daniels, M.E. 2018. Believe Bigger: Discover the Path to your Life Purpose. New York. Howard Books.

www.ingramcontent.com/pod-product-compliance
Lightning Source LLC
Chambersburg PA
CBHW030826090426
42737CB00009B/896